Michele Bachmann vs. Sarah Palin On The Issues

**Jesse Gordon,
OnTheIssues.org**

Table of Contents

Bachmann vs. Palin on International Issues 107

Book reviews 140

Bachmann vs. Palin on VoteMatch: 152

Bachmann vs. Palin
On the Issues

Representative Michele Bachmann of Minnesota and Former Governor Sarah Palin of Alaska currently stand as two of the most well-known female politicians in America today. Rep. Bachmann briefly stood as the frontrunner for the Republican presidential nomination—after winning the Iowa Straw Poll in August 2011—and Gov. Palin tops all other candidates' short-list for Vice President.

Bachmann and Palin share substantial demographic similarities: both are charismatic conservative female elected officials and Tea Party darlings. Pundits claim that Bachmann's demographic similarity to Palin contributed to Palin's declining to enter the 2012 presidential race. The pundits assume that their demographic similarity translates into interchangeability on issue stances. This book explores where that's true and where it's untrue.

We gather the two candidates' issue stances from their political autobiographies; from debates in both the 2011 election season and past elections; from public speeches; from campaign websites; and from political analysis websites. All of the excerpts appear, with many additional issue stances, on our website, www.OnTheIssues.org.

The purpose of this book, and the mission of our website, is to inform voters about candidates' issue stances—what they believe about the issues, and what they have done to implement those beliefs. The mainstream media report on candidates' politics: who's ahead this week; who "won" the last debate; who has endorsed whom. We reject the "horse race politics" that dominates the mainstream media, and instead focus on what matters: Bachmann on the issues versus Palin on the issues.

—Jesse Gordon, Editor-in-Chief, jesse@OnTheIssues.org
December 2011

Dedication

To Kathleen

Acknowledgments

This book would not have been possible without the tireless efforts of the entire OnTheIssues team: Derek Camara, Janice Gordon, Michele Gordon, Peter Hoerr, Ram Lau, Adam Leighton, Jamie Leighton, Naomi Lichtenberg, Ogden Porter, Will Rico, Dan Teittinen, Irma Teittinen, and especially Kathleen Camara.

Bachmann vs. Palin on Domestic Issues

Domestic issues focus on joint state-federal jurisdiction or enforcement, including the following topics:

- *Environment:* including pollution and EPA issues. Palin and Bachmann both believe in restricting the EPA, but have little to say on environmental issues unrelated to energy (oil issues are dealt with in our "International" section). Both agree also on restricting animal rights, defining them primarily as hunting rights.

- *Gun Control:* Both candidates extend hunting rights to an individual right to concealed carry.

- *Crime:* including mandatory sentencing and the death penalty, but neither Palin nor Bachmann focus on those issues. Their focus instead is on victims' rights.

- *Drugs:* including marijuana legalization and the War on Drugs. Also a focus for neither Palin nor Bachmann. Palin defers marijuana issues to hard drug enforcement; Bachmann defers to cross-border protection.

- *Health Care:* including federal healthcare and ObamaCare issues; plus Medicare/Medicaid and state issues. Here, we reach a core focus for both candidates: the two candidates try to outdo each other in opposing ObamaCare, both offering state-based and market-based solutions.

- *Technology and Infrastructure:* Normally this category includes local infrastructure like roads (which Palin deals with but Bachmann does not); and high-tech infrastructure policy (which Bachmann deals with but Palin does not). So we extend the definition of "infrastructure" to include "religious infrastructure" and "family infrastructure," topics which are core to both Palin's and Bachmann's political beliefs.

Michele Bachmann
on Domestic Issues

Sarah Palin
on Domestic Issues

Bachmann on Environmental Protection Agency

EPA rulemaking has been
based on politics, not science

I think it's important to note that the president recognized how devastating the EPA has been in their rulemaking, so much so that the president had to suspend current EPA rules that would have led to the shutting down of potentially 20% of all of America's coal plants.

Coal is the source that brings 45% of America's electricity. What we're seeing is that a political agenda is being advanced instead of a scientific agenda. And this is leading to massive numbers of jobs being lost.

The president told us he wanted to be like Spain when it came to green job creation, and yet Spain has one of the highest levels of unemployment. The president is bringing that here in the United States. And I think tomorrow night, when the nation tunes in to the president, I'm afraid that we won't be seeing permanent solution. I'm afraid what we'll be seeing are temporary gimmicks and more of the same that he's given before.

Source: GOP debate in Simi Valley CA at the Reagan Library,
Sep 7, 2011

Palin on Environmental Protection Agency

Sues federal EPA for misusing Endangered Species Act

As the largest and only Arctic state, we're studying climate-change. And we're suing the federal government for misusing the Endangered Species Act. There is an attempt there to use the ESA to impose environmental policies that should be debated and approved legislatively, not by court order or bureaucratic decree. Alaskans have shown through our protective laws that we're willing and able to protect our magnificent wildlife, while developing our God-given resources, by using conservation laws as they were intended. We'll challenge abuse of federal law when it's used just to lock up Alaska.

Vital projects now underway show how much science and technology have improved in a generation, greatly reducing risk to the environment. Continued work in Cook Inlet and on the North Slope, new drilling at Nikaitchug, new exploration in NPRA—these projects and more will be carried out with the safest methods.

Source: Alaska State of the State Address, Jan. 22, 2009

Bachmann on Gasoline Policy

Goal is to keep gas prices low, like $1.79 a gallon

Energy is one of the greatest opportunities for job creation that we have in the United States. We just learned today that if the federal government would pull back on all of the regulatory restrictions on American energy production, we could see 1.2 million jobs created in the United States.

We could also see created over 50 percent more American energy production. And we could also see $800 billion more revenue coming into the United States government.

Don't forget the day that President Obama took office, gasoline was $1.79 a gallon. It's entirely possible for us to get back to inexpensive energy.

The problem is, energy is too high. Let's have a goal of bringing it down because every time gasoline increases 10 cents a gallon, that's $14 billion in economic activity that every American has taken out of their pockets. This is a great solution, and this is the place to start with American job creation.

Source: GOP debate in Simi Valley CA at the Reagan Library, Sept. 7, 2011

Palin on Gasoline Policy

Resource rebate:
suspend AK 8-cent fuel tax for one year

I'm pleased to report to Alaskans that in early August, our Alaska Legislature agreed to approve a one-time resource rebate that returns part of our resource wealth to Alaskans—the owners in common of these resources. The rebate will be a direct payment of $1,200 to each Alaskan eligible for the 2008 Permanent Fund Dividend. The resource rebate was part of a larger energy package that also includes a 50% increase in the maximum loan amount for bulk fuel bridge and bulk fuel revolving loan funds to communities and cooperatives. Additionally, it suspends the state's 8-cent motor fuel tax on gasoline, marine fuel and aviation fuel for one year and strengthens the Power Cost Equalization Program.

Our lawmakers also included an additional $60 million for the Home Energy Rebate Program operated by the Alaska Housing Finance Corporation and $50 million in grant funds to the Renewable Energy Fund, bringing the total available for renewable energy projects in FY 2009 to $100 million.

Source: Alaska Governor's Office: August 2008 Newsletter, Aug. 20, 2008

Bachmann on Animal Rights

Endorsed by Sportsmen's and Animal Owners' Voting Alliance

The Sportsmen's and Animal Owners' Voting Alliance (SAOVA) is a nationwide, nonpartisan group of volunteers lobbying legislation and seeking to elect politicians who will oppose the animal rightist threat to our rights as Americans.

Candidates identified with the legend "Animal Rightist Endorsed" are the problem. They consistently vote for legislation to strip us of our rights to hunt, fish, and own pets and livestock. SAOVA ENDORSED candidates and incumbents understand the animal rightist, anti-hunting threat and have demonstrated their commitment to protecting our interests.

- 2006:6th District OPEN SEAT Michelle Bachmann (R) vs. Patty Wetterling (DFL): No basis for endorsement. Both candidates failed to answer SAOVA's questionnaire, despite extended efforts.

- 2008: 6th District Incumbent Michelle Bachmann (R) - SAOVA ENDORSED - Won.

- 2010: 6th District Incumbent Michelle Bachmann (R) - SAOVA ENDORSED.

Source: Sportsmen's and Animal Owners' Voting Alliance, SAOVA.org,
Nov 1, 2010

Palin on Animal Rights

Plenty of room for all animals—next to mashed potatoes

Not far from home, near the Talkeetna Mountains, I learned to hunt. Traveling on skis and snowshoes, we harvested ptarmigan and big game. I love meat. I eat pork chops, thick bacon burgers, and the seared fatty edges of a medium-well-done steak. But I especially love moose and caribou. I always remind people from outside our state that there's plenty of room for all Alaska's animals—right next to the mashed potatoes.

In our northern state, with some communities located hundreds of miles from big grocery stores, Alaskans have for generations lived on local, organic protein sources. Anti-hunting groups are clueless about this. It always puzzled me how some of the people who think killing and eating animals in the wild is somehow cruel have no problem buying dead animals at the grocery store, wrapped in cellophane instead of fur.

Source: Going Rogue, by Sarah Palin, p. 18-19, Nov. 17, 2009

Bachmann on Concealed Carry

National cross-state standard for concealed carry

Bachmann co-sponsored H.R.197: Establishes a national standard for the carrying of concealed firearms (other than a machinegun or destructive device) by non-residents. Authorizes a person who has a valid permit to carry a concealed firearm in one state and who is not prohibited from carrying a firearm under federal law to carry a concealed firearm in another state:

Notwithstanding any law of any State, a person who is not prohibited by Federal law from possessing a firearm and is carrying a valid license to carry a concealed firearm may carry in another State a concealed firearm.

If such other State issues licenses to carry concealed firearms, the person may carry a concealed firearm in the State under the same restrictions which apply in that State.

If such other State does not issue licenses to carry concealed firearms, the person may not carry a concealed firearm in a police station, in a courthouse, at a meeting of a governing body, in a school, at an athletic event, in an establishment licensed to dispense alcoholic beverages, or inside an airport, except to the extent expressly permitted by State law.

Source: National Right-to-Carry Reciprocity Act, HR197, Jan. 6, 2009

Palin on Concealed Carry

1997: Open carry in city library and city hall

Sarah celebrated Fourth of July 1997 by signing an administrative order that allowed the open carrying of weapons in the library. Cynics said this was an attempt to put the librarian in the crosshairs [based on Sarah's kerfuffle over pro-gay library books], but Sarah noted that the order also permitted guns to be carried or worn in City Hall.

Source: The Rogue, by Joe McGinniss, p.120, Sept. 20, 2011

1996: Allow concealed carry in bars, banks, & schools

Sarah focused the secular aspects of her campaign on two issues: closing hours for local bars and liberalization of Alaska's already lenient gun laws. The proposed changes to the state's gun laws would allow the carrying of concealed weapons in bars and banks and on school grounds—they were already permitted everywhere else. [Sarah's opponent Mayor] Stein said, "It simply wasn't a municipal issue. The state legislature would decide that, and it didn't matter how the police chief or I felt about it."

But it mattered to Sarah and her supporters. She accused Stein, a longtime member of the National Rifle Association, and the police chief, a Vietnam vet, of being "anti-gun." In Alaska—especially in Wasilla's Mat-Su Valley—this was a more serious charge than pederasty.

Source: The Rogue, by Joe McGinniss, p. 61-62, Sept. 20, 2011

Bachmann on Victims' Rights

Voted YES on expanding services for offenders' re-entry into society

H.R.1593: Second Chance Act of 2007: Community Safety Through Recidivism Prevention or the Second Chance Act: To reauthorize the grant program for reentry of offenders into the community in the Omnibus Crime Control and Safe Streets Act of 1968, and to improve reentry planning and implementation.

Proponents support voting YES because:

Rep. CONYERS: Some 650,000 men and women are leaving the Federal and State prisons each year. More than 2/3 of them are arrested for new crimes within 3 years of their release. The Second Chance Act will help provide these men and women with the training, counseling and other support needed to help them obtain & hold steady jobs; to kick their drug and alcohol habits; rebuild their families; and deal with the many other challenges that they face in their efforts to successfully rejoin society.

Opponents recommend voting NO because:

Rep. GOHMERT: The programs that are sought to be renewed are ones we don't have information on how successful they were. I can tell you from my days as a judge, there was some anecdotal evidence that it looked like faith-based programs did a better job of dramatically reducing recidivism. In addition, dismissing all charges if someone completes drug rehab under another provision I think is outrageous. You are going to remove the hammer that would allow you to keep people in line?

Source: Second Chance Act; Bill HR1593 ; vote no. 1083,Nov 13, 2007

Palin on Victims' Rights

Victims' rights are critical to "justice for all"

WHEREAS, Alaska has made great strides in ensuring crime victims are treated with dignity and respect. Victims' rights are a critical component of the promise of "justice for all," the foundation for America's justice system.

WHEREAS, crime victims in Alaska have protections and guaranties under the Alaska State Constitution, but we must do better to strive to protect, expand, and observe crime victims' rights so that there truly is justice for victims and justice for all.

NOW, THEREFORE, I, Sarah Palin, Governor of the state of Alaska, do hereby proclaim April 13-19, 2008, as Crime Victims' Rights Week in Alaska, and reaffirm this state's commitment to strive to reach the goal of justice for all by ensuring that all victims are afforded their legal rights and provided with assistance as they face the financial, physical, and psychological impact of crime.

Source: Alaska Governor's Office: Proclamation, "Crime Victims,"
Mar 18, 2008

Bachmann on the Drug War

Voted NO on more funding for Mexico to fight drugs

Congressional Summary: Merida Initiative to Combat Illicit Narcotics and Reduce Organized Crime Authorization Act: Provide assistance for Mexico for:

- counternarcotics and countertrafficking

- port & airport security to assist in controlling the Mexico-US and Mexico-Central America borders;

- intelligence gathering operational technology; and

- public security and law enforcement, including assistance to the National Council Against Addiction.

Proponent's argument to vote Yes: Rep. HOWARD BERMAN (D, CA-28): The drug crisis facing the US remains a top national security threat. This bill represents a new partnership with Mexico and Central American countries to face the immediate security threat of drug gangs, and help these neighbors build the capacity of their law enforcement agencies.

Opponent's argument to vote No: Rep. MICHAEL McCAUL (R, TX-10): We need a strategy on this side of the border: a two-pronged Approach; a comprehensive strategy that deals not only with the Mexican side but with the US side. And for too long, our border sheriffs and our Border Patrol agents have been outmanned and outgunned. And if we are going to provide assistance to Mexico, it seems to me we ought to be providing assistance to our men and women on our side fighting this war every day.

Source: Merida Initiative; Bill HR.6028 ; vote number H393, June 10, 2008

Palin on the Drug War

Opposes legalizing marijuana, but meth is greater threat

What about the social issues that Alaskans, especially the party faithful who often decide primary elections, may find important? Here's what Sarah Palin has to say about marijuana.

Palin doesn't support legalizing marijuana, worrying about the message it would send to her four kids. But when it comes to cracking down on drugs, she says methamphetamines are the greater threat and should have a higher priority.

Source: Anchorage Daily News, "Little play," by K. Hopkins, Aug. 6, 2006

Bachmann on ObamaCare

ObamaCare is unconstitutional; I'm committed to its repeal

PERRY: I will use an executive order to get rid of as much of Obamacare as I can on day one.

ROMNEY: If I'm president, on day one I'll grant a waiver from Obamacare to all 50 states.

BACHMANN: With all due respect to the governors, I've read this Obamacare health care bill, I've been fighting this fight the last couple of years. Waivers and executive orders won't cut it. If you could solve Obamacare with an executive order, any president could do it and any president could undo it. That's not how it can be done. Plus, no state has the constitutional right to force a person as a condition of citizenship to buy a product or service against their will. It's unconstitutional, whether it's the state government or whether it's the federal government. The only way to eradicate Obamacare is to pull it out by the root and branch to fully repeal it. It's the only way we're going to get rid of it. This is the election that's going to decide if we have socialized medicine in this country or not. This is it.

Source: GOP Tea Party debate in Tampa FL, Sept. 12, 2011

Palin on ObamaCare

ObamaCare should focus on helping doctors via tort reform

Congressional Democrats hatched a plan to pass the ObamaCare bill without the House ever actually voting on it! And why? Because the support in Congress wasn't there. And the support in Congress wasn't there because public support wasn't there. The American people have a principled wisdom that all the lawmakers & academics & schooled-up "experts" in DC fail to appreciate. Washington may have managed to make it law, but we still don't support ObamaCare. It turns out we can't be so easily bought.

Still, the bill was passed and the damage has been done. In the end, this unsustainable bill jeopardizes the very thing it was supposed to fix: our health care system. Somewhere along the way we forgot that health care reform is about doctors & patients, not the IRS & politicians. Instead of helping doctors with tort reform, this bill has made primary care physicians think about getting out of medicine. It was supposed to make health care more affordable, but our premiums will continue to go up.

Source: America by Heart, by Sarah Palin, p. 21, Nov. 23, 2010

Bachmann on Market-based Healthcare

End the idea that government should keep buying more stuff

Q: If you were president, would you repeal prescription drug benefits for seniors under Medicare?

BACHMANN: I think that the principle has to change, because for years, politicians have run on the idea that government is going to buy people more stuff and that the federal government would be taking care of people's prescription drugs, their retirement, their health care, their housing, their food. We're the everybody else that's paying for the freight for all of this. That's the principle that has to change, because we have to now recognize that, going forward, this isn't going to work anymore. We have to be an ownership society, where individual responsibility, personal responsibility once again becomes the animating American principle. And we can't be ashamed of that.

Source: GOP Tea Party debate in Tampa FL, Sept. 12, 2011

ObamaCare replaces finest system with government coverage

The president should repeal Obamacare and support free-market solutions, like medical malpractice reform and allowing all Americans to buy any healthcare policy they like anywhere in the United States.

Source: State of the Union Tea Party response, Jan. 26, 2011

Palin on Market-based Healthcare

Health care must be market-and business-driven

Governor Sarah Palin today introduced the Alaska Health Care Transparency Act which will provide more effective tools to help Alaskans access affordable health care, and to ensure our health care system is responsive to changing demographics and market conditions.

The bill would establish an Alaska health care information office to give consumers factual information on quality, cost and other important matters to help them make better-informed decisions about health care in the state. Recognizing that health care must be market-and business-driven, rather than restricted by government, Governor Palin is proposing a repeal of the Certificate of Need program (CON). CON is a regulatory process that requires certain health care providers to obtain state approval before offering certain new or expanded services. [Palin's administration] concluded that the CON program does not benefit the citizens of Alaska, given the litigious environment surrounding it.

Source: Alaska Governor's Office: press release, "Transparency,"
Jan 19, 2008

Bachmann on Tort Reform

Liability shield to allow charities to provide healthcare

Bachmann called for a "liability shield" for doctors to boost access to health care. The "shield" would protect health care providers from lawsuits in connection with free health care offered to those who couldn't otherwise afford it.

Bachmann said that doctors and others who once provided charity care are scared off today by the legal risks associated with it. The "liability shield" would allay those fears. "Why not do that? Why not take care of poor people?" Bachmann said. "Why not make your lives cheaper and better so you don't have to worry about health care?"

In Iowa, something very similar to such a shield is already in place. Doctors who enter into a "protection agreement" under the program receive legal defense and indemnification for care provided to uninsured and underinsured patients.

Bachmann's proposal was light on details, but ostensibly would be a federal program, conflicting with her typical health-care rhetoric, which is sharply critical of federal involvement in medicine.

Source: Jason Noble in Des Moines Register, "Bachmann charity care,"
Oct. 28, 2011

Palin on Tort Reform

ObamaCare should focus on helping doctors via tort reform

Congressional Democrats hatched a plan to pass the ObamaCare bill without the House ever actually voting on it! And why? Because the support in Congress wasn't there. And the support in Congress wasn't there because public support wasn't there. The American people have a principled wisdom that all the lawmakers & academics & schooled-up "experts" in DC fail to appreciate. Washington may have managed to make it law, but we still don't support ObamaCare. It turns out we can't be so easily bought.

Still, the bill was passed and the damage has been done. In the end, this unsustainable bill jeopardizes the very thing it was supposed to fix: our health care system. Somewhere along the way we forgot that health care reform is about doctors & patients, not the IRS & politicians. Instead of helping doctors with tort reform, this bill has made primary care physicians think about getting out of medicine. It was supposed to make health care more affordable, but our premiums will continue to go up.

Source: America by Heart, by Sarah Palin, p. 21, Nov. 23, 2010

Bachmann on Stem Cells

Human embryonic stem cell research unnecessary and unethical

I am disappointed with the President's decision to use taxpayer funds to promote unnecessary and unethical scientific procedures [including human embryonic stem cell research]. It is exciting to witness the discoveries that science has brought us, but science does not require us to enter this brave new world. In fact, science has given us options that permit progress with ethics.

Not only is it immoral to destroy human embryos, but it is even worse to place women in a position where their health is at risk to do unethical research—especially in light of the recent discoveries that adult stem cells can reprogram cells without the use of potentially cancer-causing viruses. This is a marvelous breakthrough.

I am thrilled with the advances that science has made. But in the process of protecting some lives, it is essential that we do not harm others, impact women's infertility, and endanger women's lives—all at the taxpayer's expense.

Source: Speech on House floor: stem cell research, March 9, 2009

NOTES: 'Stem Cells' are undifferentiated cells, which are useful in research for cloning and for treating many diseases. Stem cells are best taken from human fetuses; hence the pro-life opposition. Many pro-life advocates support fetal stem cell research because of the medical potential. In 2001, Pres. Bush announced that the federal policy would be to allow fetal stem cell research on existing stem cell lines but not on new ones.

Palin on Stem Cells

Stricter than McCain on stem-cell research

You and Sen. McCain have differences on some issues, McCain's vetting adviser continued. He is pro-life, but he's in favor of exceptions in the cases of rape & incest; you are not. Sen. McCain is in favor of stem cell research; you are not. We'll never ask you to make a statement that contradicts your beliefs, but we expect you to support the policies of the administration you'd be part of. And we may ask you to appear in ads advocating those positions. Do you have a problem with that?

No, I don't, not at all, Palin said.

They asked her nothing to plumb the depths of her knowledge about foreign or domestic policy. They didn't explore her preparedness to be VP. They assumed she knew as much as the average governor, and that what she didn't know, she would pick up on the fly. They weren't searching for problems. They were looking for a last-second solution.

What reassured them was Palin's preternatural calm and self-possession. Never once did she betray any jitters or lack of confusion.

Source: Game Change, by Heilemann & Halpern, p.361-362,
Jan 11, 2010

Bachmann on Christian Heritage

Recognize Christianity's importance to western civilization

Bachmann co-sponsored a Resolution recognizing Christianity's importance to western civilization:

- WHEREAS Christmas is a holiday of great significance to Americans and many other cultures;

- WHEREAS there are approximately 225,000,000 Christians in the US, making Christianity the religion of over 3/4 of the population;

- WHEREAS there are approximately 2,000,000,000 Christians throughout the world, making Christianity the largest religion in the world;

- WHEREAS the United States, being founded as a constitutional republic in the traditions of western civilization, finds much in its history that points observers back to its Judeo-Christian roots;

NOW, THEREFORE, be it Resolved, That the House of Representatives recognizes the Christian faith as one of the great religions of the world;

- Acknowledges the role played by Christians and Christianity in the founding of the US and in the formation of the western civilization; and

- Rejects bigotry and persecution directed against Christians, both in the US and worldwide.

Source: Resolution on Importance of Christmas (H.Res.847) on Dec. 6, 2007

Palin on Christian Heritage

Recognize America's historic and founding Christian heritage

• WHEREAS, the celebration of Christian Heritage Week reminds Alaskans of the role Christianity has played in our rich heritage. Many truly great men and women of America, giants in the structuring of American history, were Christians of caliber and integrity who did not hesitate to express their faith:

• WHEREAS, the Preamble to the Constitution of the State of Alaska begins with, "We the people of Alaska, grateful to God and to those who founded our nation..."

• WHEREAS, George Washington enunciated, "animated alone by the pure spirit of Christianity... we may enjoy every temporal and spiritual felicity."

• WHEREAS, James Madison, father of the United States Constitution advocated "the diffusion of the light of Christianity in our nation" in his Memorial and Remonstrance.

NOW, THEREFORE, I, Gov. Sarah Palin, do hereby proclaim October 21-27, 2007, as Alaska's 9th Annual Christian Heritage Week in Alaska, and encourage all citizens to celebrate this week.

Source: Alaska Governor's Office: Proclamation, "Christian Heritage,"
Sep 14, 2007

Bachmann on Church and State

Separation of church and state is a myth

Q: In 2006, you said that public schools are "teaching children that there is separation of church and state," and added "I am here to tell you that's a myth." Should there be limits on government's ability to inject religion into the public square?

BACHMANN: Thomas Jefferson stated it best: the US government should not be a state church. That's really the fundamental separation of church and state. When Jefferson was asked whether the US would have a national church, he said no, because we believe in freedom of conscience, we believe in freedom of religious liberty, and expression, and speech. That's a foundational principle. But that doesn't mean that we aren't people of faith, and that people of faith shouldn't be allowed to exercise religious liberty in the public square. Of course we should be able to [publicly] exercise our faith. Whether that expression occurs in a public school or occurs in a public building, we should be able to have freedom for all people to express our belief in God.

Source: GOP Google debate in Orlando FL, Sept. 22, 2011

NOTE: The US Constitution does not mandate "separation of church and state." That phrase comes from a letter written by Thomas Jefferson while President, in 1802. The Constitution's "Establishment Clause" says that the US will have no state church (known as an "established religion"), which has been interpreted to mean the federal government cannot fund one church over another.

Palin on Church and State

OpEd: Core values defined by political ambition plus church

Q: What are Sarah Palin's core principles and values?

A: Her values are those of her church: evangelical Christian fundamentalism. In Alaska, social life in small towns revolves around church membership: it's too cold usually to hang out in the back yard with neighbors; many people work for very small family businesses; so the church is the main source of social life and is also a replacement for extended family—many people in Alaska are from somewhere else. As a result, the teachings of a church are reinforced repeatedly throughout the week. And people socialize with fellow congregants. So, the values of one's particular church typically shape the values of the person and the individual's social circle. However, like all successful politicians, she is willing to set aside her core values in order to further her political ambition. As governor, Sarah Palin set aside her personal objections to abortion, to homosexuality, etc., and did not take action to get creationism taught in the schools.

Source: Phone interview with Anne Kilkenny, resident of Wasilla AK,
Sep 21, 2008

Bachmann on Husband's Role

Bible's "be submissive to husband" means mutual respect

Q: In 2006, when you were running for Congress, you described a moment in your life when your husband said you should study for a degree in tax law. You said you hated the idea. And then you explained, "But the Lord said, 'Be submissive. Wives, you are to be submissive to your husbands.'" As president, would you be submissive to your husband?

A: Marcus and I will be married for 33 years this September 10th. I'm in love with him. And what submission means to us, it means respect. I respect my husband. He's a wonderful, godly man, and a great father. And he respects me as his wife. That's how we operate our marriage. We respect each other. We love each other. And I've been so grateful that we've been able to build a home together. We have five wonderful children and 23 foster children. We've built a business together and a life together And I'm very proud of him.

Source: Iowa Straw Poll GOP debate in Ames Iowa, Aug. 11, 2011

Palin on Husband's Role

Raises kids with network of relatives, plus Todd as Mr. Mom

Q: McCain likes to get up early in the morning and go. And you?

A: Morning person. Yup. We don't sleep much. Too much to do. What I've had to do, though, is in the middle of the night, put down the BlackBerries and pick up the breast pump. Do a couple of things different and still get it all done.

Q: As a new mom, how are you going to juggle all this?

A: I am thankful to be married to a man who loves being a dad as much as I love being a mom, so he is my strength. And practically speaking, we have a great network of help with lots of grandparents and aunties and uncles all around us. We have a lot of help.

Q: So will your husband be on leave now indefinitely to be Mr. Mom?

A: I would say so, yes.

Source: Sandra Sobieraj Westfall in People magazine, Aug. 29, 2008

Bachmann on Her Children

Raised 23 foster kids, with her own kids, as "treatment home"

Mrs. Bachmann has offered few details about her foster children, and for privacy reasons their names have never been made public. Over time, Mrs. Bachmann's husband has said, their home grew so full that they expanded their kitchen. In choosing to leave work, she said, "I finally realized my dream, which was to be mom of a big, happy family."

The Bachmanns were licensed by the state from 1992 to 2000 to handle up to three foster children at a time; the last child arrived in 1998. They began by offering short-term care for girls with eating disorders who were treated through a program at the University of Minnesota, said the CEO of the private agency that handled the placements. He said the Bachmann home was "technically considered a treatment home," which offered a higher level of reimbursement. Critics point out that the couple had not "raised" the children, as Mrs. Bachmann has said. But, the CEO said, "From our agency's perspective, I thought they did a very nice job."

Source: Sheryl Gay Stolberg in New York Times, June 21, 2011

Palin on Her Children

On Down baby: God won't give me something I can't handle

I never planned on being the mother of a son with special needs. I thought, "God will never give me something I can't handle." And when I found out that my baby would be born with Down syndrome, I thought immediately, "Hey God, remember you promised you wouldn't give me something I couldn't handle? Well, I don't think I can handle this." This wasn't part of my life's plan, and I was scared.

I didn't know if my heart was ready. I didn't know if I was patient and nurturing enough.

But when Trig was born I understood that God DID know what he was doing! What at first seemed like an overwhelming challenge has turned into our greatest blessing. All the time, it seems that God was whispering in my ear and saying, "Are you going to trust me? Are you going to walk the walk or just talk the talk?" But when they laid Trig in my arms & he just kind of melted into my chest, he seemed to say to me, "See, Mom, God knows what he's doing. He gave me to you, and you to me, and this is going to be a wonderful journey."

Source: America by Heart, by Sarah Palin, p.153-154, Nov. 23, 2010

Bachmann vs. Palin
on Economic Issues

Economic issues focus on the recession recovery and all fiscal matters, including the following topics:

- *Budget & Economy:* including deficit spending and all aspects of the federal budget. Rep. Bachmann's policies are federally oriented (as provider of the economic stimulus); Gov. Palin's are state oriented (as recipient of the economic stimulus).

- *Tax Reform:* including income taxes, tax rates, and bracket redistribution. The two candidates agree on eliminating the death tax; on reducing the capital gains tax; and on a philosophy of reducing taxes.

- *Corporations:* including corporate taxation and corporate welfare. Bachmann and Palin agree on reducing corporate taxes. They also agree on fighting crony capitalism, but do not associate that with corporate welfare at all. .

- *Jobs:* including unemployment and union issues, but not the underlying economic sources of job growth and loss (that's covered in the economic issues section). The two candidates agree on restricting unions, and agree that high unemployment is the Democrat's fault.

- *Government Reform:* Palin & Bachmann agree on more transparency and both claim to want to reduce earmarks. But Bachmann opposes whistleblower protection while Palin was a whistleblower.

- *Social Security:* including the current Trust Fund and changes for the future. Bachmann supports opt-out mechanisms; Palin supports a state-run retirement supplement.

Michele Bachmann on Economic Issues

Sarah Palin
on Economic Issues

Bachmann on Economic Stimulus

Voted YES on $192B additional
anti-recession stimulus spending

- $7 billion Increase in Fund balance appropriation (without fiscal year limitation).

- Increases from $315 billion to $400 billion the maximum loan principal for FY2009 commitments to guarantee single family loans insured under the Mutual Mortgage Insurance Fund (MMIF).

- Increases from $300 billion to $400 billion the limit on new Government National Mortgage Association guarantees.

Proponent's argument to vote Yes: Rep. LEWIS (D, GA-5): This bipartisan bill will provide the necessary funds to keep important transportation projects operating in States around the country. The Highway Trust Fund will run out of funding by September. We must act, and we must act now.

Opponent's argument to vote No: Rep. CAMP (R, MI-4): [This interim spending is] needed because the Democrats' economic policy has resulted in record job loss, record deficits, and none of the job creation they promised. We had a choice when it came to the stimulus last February. We could have chosen a better policy of stimulating private-sector growth creating twice the jobs at half the price. That was the Republican plan. Instead, Democrats insisted on their government focus plan, which has produced no jobs and a mountain of debt.

Source: Omnibus Appropriations Act Amendment; Bill H.R. 3357 ;
vote number H659 on July 29, 2009

Palin on Economic Stimulus

"No thank you" to federal dollars with fat strings attached

The Obama administration's mammoth $787 billion stimulus package is a good example of bribing the states to surrender their rights. As governor of Alaska, I angered a lot of state bureaucrats when I turned down a chunk of the federal money slated for Alaska in Obama's stimulus bill. I accepted the money that would go to create construction projects and provide needed medical care to the disadvantaged, but I said, "no, thank you" to dollars that had fat federal strings attached to them.

The debt-ridden, unsustainable stimulus scheme disrespected the Tenth Amendment by attempting to bribe the states with money in exchange for more Washington control. The money would have gone to fund government, not real jobs in the private sector. Embarrassingly, the Republican-controlled state legislature overrode my veto and Alaska accepted the funds. And now, to pay for them, Alaskans will have to put up with even more rule-making from Washington.

Source: America by Heart, by Sarah Palin, p. 76-77, Nov. 23, 2010

FactCheck: No, Alaska doesn't deny federal stimulus help

THE FACTS: Alaska is also one of the states most dependent on federal subsidies, receiving much more assistance from Washington than it pays in federal taxes. A study for the nonpartisan Tax Foundation found that in 2005, the state received $1.84 for every dollar it sent to Washington.

Source: AP Fact Check about "Going Rogue," in NY Times, Nov. 13, 2009

Bachmann on Mortgage Crisis

Subprime mortgage crisis due to errors by feds, not banks

Q: Do you think it's right that no Wall Street executives have gone to jail for the damage they did to the economy?

A: If you look at the problem with the economic meltdown, you can trace it right back to the federal government, because it was the federal government that demanded that banks and mortgage companies lower platinum-level lending standards to new lows.

Q: But the federal government had also deregulated them.

A: It was the federal government that pushed the subprime loans. It was the federal government that pushed the Community Reinvestment Act, and government-directed housing goals. They pushed the banks to meet these rules. And if banks failed to meet those rules, then the federal government said, we won't let you merge; we won't let you grow. There's a real problem: We had artificially low interest rates. Freddie and Fannie were the center of the universe on the mortgage meltdown, and we had lending standards lowered for the first time in American history.

Source: GOP debate at Dartmouth College, NH, Oct. 11, 2011

Palin on Mortgage Crisis

Predatory lenders got us into the housing crisis

Q: Who is to blame for the subprime lending meltdown?

PALIN: It was predator lenders who tried to talk Americans into thinking that it was smart to buy a $300,000 house if we could only afford a $100,000 house. There was deception, and there was greed and there is corruption. Joe Six Pack, hockey moms across the nation, we need to band together and say never again. We need to demand from the federal government strict oversight of those entities in charge of our investments and our savings. Let's do what our parents told us before we probably even got that first credit card. Don't live outside of our means.

BIDEN: Barack warned about the subprime mortgage crisis. We let Wall Street run wild. John McCain thought the answer is that tried and true Republican response, deregulate, deregulate. And guess what? The middle class needs tax relief. They need it now.

Source: Vice Presidential debate against Joe Biden, Oct. 2, 2008

Bachmann on Balanced Budget

Balanced Budget Amendment with 3/5 vote to override

Bachmann signed H.J.RES.1:

Constitutional Amendment to prohibit outlays for a fiscal year (except those for repayment of debt principal) from exceeding total receipts for that fiscal year (except those derived from borrowing) unless Congress, by a three-fifths rollcall vote of each chamber, authorizes a specific excess of outlays over receipts.

- Requires a three-fifths rollcall vote of each chamber to increase the public debt limit.

- Directs the President to submit a balanced budget to Congress annually.

- Prohibits any bill to increase revenue from becoming law unless approved by a majority of each chamber by rollcall vote.

- Authorizes waivers of these provisions when a declaration of war is in effect or under other specified circumstances involving military conflict.

- Amendment to the Constitution shall be valid when ratified by the legislatures of three-fourths of the several States within seven years after the date of its submission for ratification

Joint Resolution for Amendment to the Constitution HJR1 on Jan. 6, 2009

Palin on Balanced Budget

Top priorities for AK include ethics & balanced budget

"One hundred days ago, I outlined my top priorities for the state: a natural gasline, a balanced budget including temporary relief for the unexpected PERS/TRS burden, ethics reform, and workforce development," said Governor Palin. "I am proud of our accomplishments to date, but we still have a lot of work to do."

Source: Alaska Governor's Office: press release, "100th Day,"
Mar 13, 2007

Top priorities for AK include ethics & balanced budget

When our families, when our small businesses, we start running our finances in to the red, what do we do? We tighten our belts and we cut back budgets. That is what we teach our children, to live within our means. That is what Todd and I do when we have to make payroll, buy new equipment for our commercial fishing business. We have to plan for the future, meet a budget.

But in Washington, why is it just the opposite of that? This week, they unveiled a record busting, mind boggling $3.8 trillion federal budget and they keep borrowing and they keep printing these dollars and they keep making us more and more beholden to foreign countries and they keep making us take these steps towards insolvency. Now what they are doing in proposing these big new programs with giant price tags, they're sticking our kids with the bill. And that is immoral. That is generational theft. We are stealing the opportunities from our children.

Source: Tea Party Convention speeches, Feb. 6, 2010

Bachmann on Limited Taxation

What you earn is your money, not the government's

Q: Out of every dollar I earn, how much do you think that I deserve to keep?

A: BACHMANN: I think you earned every dollar. You should get to keep every dollar that you earn. That's your money; that's not the government's money. That's the whole point. Barack Obama seems to think that when we earn money, it belongs to him and we're lucky just to keep a little bit of it. I don't think that at all. I think when people make money, it's their money.

Obviously, we have to give money back to the government s that we can run the government, but we have to have a completely different mindset. And that mindset is, the American people are the genius of this economy. It certainly isn't government that's the genius. And that's the two views.

Pres. Obama has embraced a view of government-directed temporary fixes and gimmicks. They don't work. He's destroyed the economy. What does work is private solutions that are permanent in the private sector. That gives certainty; that will grow our economy.

Source: GOP Google debate in Orlando FL, Sept. 22, 2011

Palin on Limited Taxation

Core GOP belief is limited government and limited taxation

Q: At the convention here, we have at least three people I know who are running for Congress; what questions would you ask them to determine whether or not you would support them?

A: I'm going to ask them if they think that we're taxed enough already. And if they say yes, I'm going to say well what are you going to do about it. Because really, we don't want to just hear the talk. We want to know that they walk the walk, either via a record that perhaps they can prove to us in other elected office they have had. But if they feel that they've been taxed enough already and that they make us a commitment that they are going to do something about it and if they just believe in that constitutional limited government [that's important. There are] things on the periphery that perhaps I wouldn't agree with very single aspect of their agenda, but they have got the basics down, I think it would be wise for us to be supportive.

Source: Tea Party Convention Q&A, Feb. 6, 2010

Bachmann on Death Tax and Capital Gains

Repeal tax hikes in capital gains

Bachmann signed the Contract From America, clause 10: Stop the Tax Hikes:

Permanently repeal all tax hikes, including those to the income, capital gains, and death taxes, currently scheduled to begin in 2011.

Source: The Contract From America, July 8, 2010

Repeal the Death Tax

A BILL to repeal the Federal estate and gift taxes:

Subtitle B of the Internal Revenue Code of 1986 (relating to estate, gift, and generation-skipping taxes) is hereby repealed.

The repeal shall apply to estates of decedents dying, gifts made, and generation-skipping transfers made after the date of the enactment of this Act.

Source: Death Tax Repeal Act HR205 on Jan. 6, 2009

Palin on Death Tax and Capital Gains

To end recession: slay the death tax and cut capital gains

Our nation is facing great challenges, but I'm optimistic—ad I know there is a way forward.

Ronald Reagan faced an even worse recession. He showed us how to get out of one. If you want real job growth, cut capital gains taxes and slay the death tax once and for all. And if we really want to help the poor and middle class get through this recession, how about cutting their payroll taxes? Giving people control over more of the money they've earned: now that's real stimulus. Get federal spending under control, and then set aside and watch this economy roar back to life.

The way forward is full of promise. But it takes more courage for a politician to step back and let the free market correct itself than it does to push through quick fixes. Reagan showed courage when he stayed the course through the long recession of the early 1980s. Critics even in his own party told him to abandon his tax cuts. He was confident they would work. And they did.

Source: Going Rogue, by Sarah Palin, p.391-392, Nov. 17, 2009

Bachmann on Corporate Tax

High corporate taxes lead to jobs leaving the country

Q: How can you create jobs as quickly as possible?

A: Taxes lead to jobs leaving the country. We have the second highest corporate tax rate in the world. If you go back to 1981, we had a lot of high corporate tax countries. It was 47% on average on a lot of countries across the world. But if you look today in the US, we have an effective rate if you average in state taxes, with federal taxes, of about 40%. But the world took a clue, because capital is mobile, and capital went to places where corporate tax rates went to 25% and falling. We're still stuck in a 1986 era of about a 40% tax rate. We have to lower the tax rate because it's a cost of doing business, but we have to do so much more than that. Our biggest problem right now is our regulatory burden.

Source: CNBC GOP Primary debate in Rochester MI, Nov. 9, 2011

Reducing repatriation tax to zero would bring in $1.2T

The president wanted to borrow money from countries like China to pay it back for a stimulus. We've got $1.2 trillion already that's been earned by American countries overseas. If we have a 0 percent tax rate, we can bring that $1.2 trillion—it's called repatriation—bring that in. You'd have 1.2 trillion flooded into the system, then pass the free trade agreements so that we can move the economy, permanently lower the tax code. I'm a federal tax lawyer. I know how to do that.

Source: GOP Tea Party debate in Tampa FL, Sept. 12, 2011

Palin on Corporate Tax

Under Obama plan,
small businesses will see tax increases

PALIN: When you talk about Barack's plan to tax increase affecting only those making $250,000 a year or more, you're forgetting millions of small businesses that are going to fit into that category. So they're going to be the ones paying higher taxes thus resulting in fewer jobs being created and less productivity. Patriotic is saying, government, you're not always the solution. In fact, too often you're the problem so, government, lessen the tax burden and get out of the way and let the private sector and our families grow.

BIDEN: No one making less than $250,000 under Obama's plan will see one penny of their tax raised. And 95% percent of the people making less than $150,000 will get a tax break. John wants to add new tax cuts for corporate America and the very wealthy while giving nothing to the middle class. We have a different value set. The middle class is the economic engine. They deserve the tax breaks, not the wealthy who are doing well.

Source: Vice Presidential debate against Joe Biden, Oct. 2, 2008

Bachmann on Small Business

We need to give job creators certainty

Q: Doesn't Obama's jobs plan put everybody's feet to the fire?

A: He kept saying, "Hurry, hurry." How many times did he say, "Pass the plan"? I hope Congress doesn't pass this plan!

Q: What don't you like?

A: I think what's very unfortunate in all of this and what the coming days will show is that the people who are the job creators—I'm one of them, a job creator in our own small business—this is—this doesn't tell a job creator that we'll see certainty. This doesn't tell a creator that the return on their investment is bound to be safe. Obama's speech will impress no one who has an ability to be able to bring the economy back because the real problem in all this is that Washington, D.C., will never solve the economy! It's Main Street that solves it. Washington just messes it up and gets in the way.

Source: Response to Obama's 2011 Jobs Speech on Fox News "On The Record," Sept. 8, 2011

Palin on Small Business

Small businesses have to be brave enough to fail

I considered the Obama administration's panicky effort to stimulate the economy by spending enormous amounts of borrowed money shortsighted and ill-conceived. It defied the lessons of history and common sense. His nearly $1 trillion stimulus package was patently unfair both to future generations who will inherit our wasteful debt and to the everyday Americans who work very hard to pay the taxes that the administration seeks to spend at breakneck speed.

"Bristol, answer me this," I said to my daughter. "You want to buy a coffee show someday, right? You know you'll be rewarded for your hard work to meet a demand for a quality product and good service. And you know you'll have to be brave enough to fail, right? This business would be YOUR responsibility. You can't look to anyone to bail out if you make poor decisions" I told Bristol, "Don't do it until this administration understands government's role in private business. Or wait until they're out of office."

Source: Going Rogue, by Sarah Palin, p.357-358, Nov. 17, 2009

Bachmann on Lobbyist Transparency

Voted YES on requiring lobbyist disclosure of bundled donations

Amends the Lobbying Disclosure Act of 1995 to require a registered lobbyist who bundles contributions totaling over $5,000 to one covered recipient in one quarter to:

• file a quarterly report with Congress; and

• notify the recipient.

• "Covered recipient" includes federal candidates, political party committees, or leadership PACs.

Proponents support voting YES because: This measure will more effectively regulate, but does not ban, the practice of registered lobbyists bundling together large numbers of campaign contributions. "Bundling" contributions which the lobbyist physically receives and forwards to the candidate, or which are credited to the lobbyist through a specific tracking system put in place by the candidate. This bill requires quarterly reporting on bundled contributions. We ultimately need to move to assist the public financing of campaigns, as soon as we can. But until we do, the legislation represents an extremely important step forward.

Opponents support voting NO because: Why are [non-leadership] PACs omitted from the disclosure requirements in this legislation? Why should political party committees be exposed to more sunshine, but not PACs? The fact that PACs give more money to Democrats is not the only answer. What the American people want is more honesty and more accountability.

Source: Honest Leadership and Open Government Act; Bill H R 2316 ; vote number 2007-423 on May 24, 2007

Palin on Lobbyist Transparency

Transparency meetings should not be held behind closed doors

Remember our administration promise that it would be good stewards of taxpayer dollars. Remember? Remember Vice President Biden? He was put in charge of a tough, unprecedented oversight effort. That's how it was introduced. You know why? Because nobody messes with Joe.

Now, this was all part of that hope and change and transparency. And now a year later, I got to ask the supporters of all that, how is that hopey-changey stuff working out for you?

See, I tried to look into that transparency thing, but Joe's meetings with the transparency and accountability board, it was closed to the public. Yes. They held a transparency meeting behind closed doors.

So I'm not sure if anybody's messing with Joe. But here is what I do know. A lot of that stimulus cash, it ended up in some pretty odd places, including districts that didn't even exist.

Source: Tea Party Convention speeches, Feb. 6, 2010

Bachmann on Earmark Reform

Moratorium on all earmarks until budget is balanced

Bachmann signed the Contract From America, clause 9: "Stop the Pork:"

Place a moratorium on all earmarks until the budget is balanced, and then require a 2/3 majority to pass any earmark.

Source: The Contract From America, on July 8, 2010

Identify constitutionality in every new congressional bill

Bachmann signed the Contract From America, clause 1: "Protect the Constitution:"

Require each bill to identify the specific provision of the Constitution that gives Congress the power to do what the bill does.

Source: The Contract From America, on July 8, 2010

Palin on Earmark Reform

Supported "Bridge to Nowhere"; now criticizes it

Although she would later criticize Congressional earmarks like Alaska's infamous "Bridge to Nowhere," proposed for the town of Ketchikan at a cost of about $400 million, as mayor she began the practice of making annual trips to Washington to press for them on behalf of their town.

Source: New York Times, pp. A1 & A10, "An Outsider Who Charms," Aug. 29, 2008

Fight "bridge to nowhere" and all earmarks

[On earmark reform], here in Alaska, our administration canceled that "bridge to nowhere." We know that that earmark wasn't in the nation's best interest. So we're going to be a part of that reform also. It's absolutely necessary or the Republican agenda which I do believe is the right agenda for Alaska and for [America].

Source: CNBC "Kudlow & Company" Interview, July 31, 2008

Supports state funding for Gravina Island bridge

Q: Would you continue state funding for the proposed Knik Arm and Gravina Island bridges? [Note: The Gravina Island bridge later became known as the "Bridge to Nowhere"]

A: Yes. I would like to see Alaska's infrastructure projects built sooner rather than later. The window is now—while our congressional delegation is in a strong position to assist.

Source: Anchorage Daily News: gubernatorial candidate profile, Oct. 22, 2006

Bachmann on Whistleblower Policy

Voted NO on protecting whistleblowers from employer recrimination

Expands the types of whistleblower disclosures protected from personnel reprisals for federal employees, particularly on national security issues.

Proponents support voting YES because: This bill would strengthen one of our most important weapons against waste, fraud and abuse, and that is Federal whistleblower protections. One of the most important provisions protects national security whistleblowers. There are a lot of Federal officials who knew the intelligence on Iraq was wrong. But none of these officials could come forward. If they did, they could have been stripped of their security clearances, or they could have been fired. Nobody blew the whistle on the phony intelligence that got us into the Iraq war.

Opponents support voting NO because: It is important that personnel within the intelligence community have appropriate opportunities to bring matters to Congress so long as the mechanisms to do so safeguard highly sensitive classified information and programs. The bill encourages intelligence community personnel to report highly sensitive intelligence matters to committees other than the Intelligence Committees. The real issue is one of protecting highly classified intelligence programs. This bill would make every claim of a self-described whistleblower, whether meritorious or not, subject to extended and protracted litigation.

Source: Honest Leadership and Open Government Act; Bill H R 2316 ;
vote number 423 on May 24, 2007

Palin on Whistleblower Policy

Gained political prominence as a whistleblower

One commentator noted that] Palin—a 44-year-old former small-town mayor who gained prominence as a whistleblower against fellow Republicans in Alaska—seemed to better suit McCain's style. "This is a maverick picking a maverick, and I think it makes sense," he said.

Source: Boston Globe, "Romney backers," p. A12, Aug. 30, 2008

OpEd: Darling of the Democrats
for taking on GOP incumbent

[An Alaska resident writes in an epilogue entitled "A View From Alaska"]:

Democrats forget when Palin was the Darling of the Democrats, because as soon as Palin took the governor's office away from a fellow Republican and tough SOB, Frank Murkowski, she tore into the Republican's "Corrupt Bastards Club" (CBC) and sent it packing, [some to jail]. The Democrats reacted by skipping around the yard and throwing confetti. Name another governor in this country who has ever done anything similar.

Source: Going Rogue, by Sarah Palin, p.405-406, Nov. 17, 2009

Bachmann on Term Limits

Promises to serve only one term as President

When was the last time someone became President and decided, without pressure, to serve only one term? Michele Bachmann's decision is a bold move that underlines her commitment to immediately make an impact as President, quickly. Bachmann's promise provides voters with a clear choice: Give Obama one more term to fix things vs. Give Bachmann one term to fix things. Voters might be more willing to take a chance with Bachmann, rather than giving Obama another four years to disappoint them.

Source: Why She Will Win, by Ron Paul Jones, p. 23, June 8, 2011

NOTES on term limits:

- The Constitution limits the president to two terms, or a total of 10 years. There are not limits for the US House or the US Senate.

- In March 1998, the Supreme Court let stand term limits for state lawmakers, but previously ruled that establishing such restrictions nationally would require amending the Constitution. Efforts to limit federal Congressional terms died out in early 1997.

- 18 states have laws limiting politicians' terms, and in 1998, more than 200 state legislators were forced to retire.

Palin on Term Limits

1996 mayoral election focus:
ideology, term limits, religion

In 1996, Sarah Palin ran for mayor and Wasilla got its first local lesson in wedge politics. The traditional turning points that had decided municipal elections in this town of less than 7,000 people— Should we pave the dirt roads? Put in sewers? Which candidate is your hunting buddy?—seemed all but obsolete the year Palin, then 32, challenged the three-term incumbent, John Stein.

Anti-abortion fliers circulated. Ms. Palin played up her church work and her membership in the National Rifle Association. The state Republican Party, never involved before because city elections are nonpartisan, ran advertisements on Ms. Palin's behalf.

"Sarah comes in with all this ideological stuff, and I was like, 'Whoa,'" said Mr. Stein, who lost the election. "But that got her elected: abortion, gun rights, term limits and the religious born-again thing. I'm not a churchgoing guy, and that was another issue: 'We will have our first Christian mayor.'"

Source: William Yardley in NY Times, "Not Politics as Usual"

Sept. 2, 2008

Bachmann on Crony Capitalism

Washington is the epicenter of crony capitalism

Q: In one of the last debates, you were asked what you would do about foreclosures, and you told moms to hang on. But your advice was let the economy recover. So do you agree with Governor Romney that the way to fix the housing market is to let the foreclosure process proceed more rapidly?

A: I agree that we have got to stop what we're doing now. When we had the financial meltdown, 50% of the homes are being financed by Fannie and Freddie. Today it's 90% of the homes. In other words, the government is the backer of the homes. Freddie and Fannie just applied this week for another $13 billion bailout because they're failing. But what did they do? They just gave bonuses of almost $13 million to 10 top executives. This is the epicenter of crony capitalism. That's what's wrong with Washington, D.C. That's lunacy. We need to put them back into bankruptcy and get them out of business. They're destroying the housing market.

Source: CNBC GOP Primary debate in Rochester MI, Nov. 9. 2011

Palin on Crony Capitalism

I fought against crony capitalism as governor

Government is taking over more and more of the role that the free market has traditionally played in America. The problem is that when government is calling the shots, it's politics that matters, not good ideas, hard work, or perseverance.

It's called crony capitalism, and it's something I fought against as governor. In Alaska, we took on "Big Oil" and its allies in government who were taking the 49th state for a ride. My administration challenged lax rules that allowed corruption and irresponsible resource development, and we even took on the largest corporation in the world at the time, Exxon-Mobil.

Our reforms helped reduce politicians' ability to play favorites and helped clean up corruption. "Big Oil," including executives and lobbyists of BP, Exxon, Conoco-Phillips, and others, didn't pal around with me, but, then, that was a mutual decision.

Source: America by Heart, by Sarah Palin, p. 84-85, Nov. 23, 2010

Bachmann on Unemployment Policy

Longer unemployment means people less likely to find jobs

Q: What did you think of the president's speech tonight [on the American Jobs Act]?

A: Well, it wasn't a plan, it was a political speech. And I think—my bottom line is, so what's new about what we heard? The president gave no new ideas. And I think the real problem is that, again, this was political. We need to do what works because quite simply, to extend payroll tax deductions—there's no credible supporting evidence that shows that created any new jobs. Not only that, extending the unemployment benefits—if you look at the president's own new economic adviser, he said in two different studies that the longer you keep people on unemployment, the less likely it is they're going to find a job. That doesn't work. More stimulus? Do we really need "son of stimulus"? We passed a trillion dollars in stimulus. Will billions more do the job? There is nothing new here!

Source: Response to 2011 Jobs Speech on Fox News "On The Record," Sept. 8, 2011

Palin on Unemployment Policy

Unemployment is higher than promised, and growing

The White House can't even tell us how many jobs were actually created. Depending on who you ask, it is anywhere from thousands to two million. But one number we are sure of is the unemployment number. That is 9.7, which is well above the 8% mark that we were promised our stimulus package would go to avoid. And unemployment now is 16.5%. You have got all these people who have given up. and they are not even enrolling in some of these programs. Tough to count them. Is that hope? Nope. It's not hope.

Source: Tea Party Convention speeches, Feb. 6, 2010

Bailout should be about job creation, not just healthcare

I, like every American I'm speaking with, we're all about this position that we have been put in, where it is the taxpayers looking to bail out. But ultimately, what the bailout does is help those who are concerned about the health care reform that is needed to help shore up our economy. It's got to be about job creation, too. Shoring up our economy, and getting it back on the right track. So health care reform and reining in spending has got to accompany tax reductions, and tax relief for Americans, and trade. We have got to see trade as opportunity, not as a competitive scar We've got to look at that as more opportunity. All of those things under the umbrella of job creation."

Source: ABC Nightly News, Sept. 25, 2008

Bachmann on Union Policy

NRLB shouldn't stop Boeing's factory
in right-to-work state

In May 2011, the National Labor Relations Board (NLRB) issued a complaint against the Boeing Company aimed at stopping the opening of a new airplane plant that Boeing had built—at a cost of some $750 million—in South Carolina. The plant was built to expand production of Boeing's new 787 "Dreamliner" passenger jet, creating 4,000 new jobs. Yet the NRLB, fired up by new Obama appointees, filed suit to stop the production, accusing Boeing of engaging in "unfair labor practice" by opening a plant in right-to-work S.C. as opposed to pro-union Washington state.

S.C.'s new governor, Nikki Haley, denounced the action: "This is a direct assault on everything we know America to be." She was right.<p>A further absurdity: the NRLB said that Boeing was taking assets away from Washington state, [but] Boeing was continuing to make 787s at a unionized plant in Everett WA; it was simply planning on building more 787s at the second plant in S.C. And because Boeing currently had backlogged orders of some 850 planes, both plants had many years of full capacity production to look forward to.

The NRLB was operating as a rogue agency, pushing beyond its authorized functions, pushing beyond liberalism, beyond activism, all the way to "unlawful."

Source: Core of Conviction, by Michele Bachmann, p.194-195
Nov. 21, 2011

Palin on Union Policy

Unions should get member permission for political donations

Q: Do you support legislation requiring labor unions to obtain permission from their members before using dues for political purposes?

A: Yes, unions represent their workers and as such, should be accountable to them.

Source: Eagle Forum 2006 Gubernatorial Candidate Questionnaire, July 31, 2006

Leverage job-training dollars thru voc-tech curriculum

I will leverage job-training dollars through efficiencies in government, private sector partnerships, and responsible investments in job training opportunities that result in good jobs for Alaskans. I look forward to working with a cross section of citizen advisors who represent private sector employers' educational institutions, union and non-union training programs and other workforce development professionals on the Alaska Workforce Investment Board. With their advice, we can meet the rapidly growing need for trained workers. I am a strong proponent of vocational and technical curriculum in our schools and will focus on this area to get our workforce ready for the future. I don't want to see an importation of Alaska's workforce when we have untapped talent here in the state, anxious for training and anxious for the opportunity to work.

Source: Palin-Parnell campaign booklet: New Energy for Alaska, Nov. 3, 2006

Bachmann on Social Security

Wean everybody off Social Security and Medicare

Rep. Michele Bachmann (R-MN) is putting forward a very daring proposal for how to fix Social Security and Medicare. Bachmann spoke this past weekend at the right-wing Constitutional Coalition in St. Louis, Missouri, and put forth her plan:

"So, what you have to do, is keep faith with the people that are already in the system, that don't have any other options, we have to keep faith with them. But basically what we have to do is wean everybody else off," said Bachmann. "And wean everybody off because we have to take those unfunded net liabilities off our bank sheet, we can't do it. So we just have to be straight with people."

Source: Eric Kleefeld on TalkingPointsMemo.com, Feb. 9, 2010

Young should invest retirement money, not give it to government

I am all in favor of everyone having a safe and solid retirement, but I wonder if the current system was the best way to achieve that goal. I learned about the illusion that each of us had his or her own Social Security account; we had no such thing. Instead, all the money went into a big general fund, allowing the politicians to do whatever they wanted with it. The government wasn't investing my retirement money at all. The government was spending it on current recipients.

Source: Core of Conviction, by Michele Bachmann, pp. 66-7, Nov. 21, 2011

Palin on Social Security

Sacrifice now to keep system for the future

Q: Should we make any changes in Social Security?

A: We are going to have to make some tough decisions today. Thomas Paine, one of our Founders, had said, 'If there is to be trouble, let it be in my day, so that my child may have peace.' What he meant way back then was that there should be an expectation that some sacrifices will have to be made, in our generation, so that future generations can have the opportunities that we've had to grow and thrive and prosper, so that our private sector can do what a private sector does best in creating jobs. So, yeah, with some practical things that have to be made, some decisions here, with perhaps changing, in future years, not adversely affecting those who are reliant on retirement benefits today, for instance, Social Security benefits, but changing, perhaps, the eligibility in future years. That has to be something that we're brave enough, courageous enough, to start talking about."

Source: NewsMax interview, Oct. 6, 2010

Fund the Seniors Longevity Bonus Program

I support funding our Seniors Longevity Bonus Program so the program can phase out on schedule, in agreement with public discussion years ago. The program was declining and it was a shame to see our esteemed pioneers face broken promises when they were prematurely lopped off the program

Source: Campaign website, www.palinforgovernor.com, "Issues," Nov. 7, 2006

Bachmann vs. Palin on Social Issues

Social issues focus on matters which are based primarily on moral values, including the following topics:

- *Abortion:* including state-level restrictions and adoption. This topic has always been the most viewed topic on our websitewww. OnTheIssues.org, so we explore several aspects. Bachmann and Palin agree on a strong pro-life stance.

- *Civil Rights:* including gay rights and minority rights. For the 2012 race, gay rights will dominate this category. Both candidates agree on opposing gay rights, but disagree on the value of feminism.

- *Education:* including charters, school vouchers, and religion in schools. Palin and Bachmann both support charters, but only Bachmann supports vouchers. They further disagree on evolution and NCLB.

- *Families and Children:* including family values in general ; but these two candidates focus on traditional marriage.

- *Welfare and Poverty:* including homelessness, welfare payments, and other poverty programs, but not a focus for either candidate.

- *Principles and Values:* including religious issues, personal issues, and partisan issues. Bachmann founded the Congressional Tea Party caucus, and Palin is also a Tea Party favorite

Michele Bachmann on Social Issues

Sarah Palin
on Social Issues

Bachmann on Right to Life

Life is the first right; I'm 100% pro-life from conception

Q: [to Bachmann]: Gov. Pawlenty says he opposes abortion rights except in cases of rape, incest, or when the mother's life is at stake. Do you have any problem with that position?

BACHMANN: I am 100 percent pro-life. I've given birth to five babies, an I've taken 23 foster children into my home. I believe in the dignity of life from conception until natural death. I believe in the sanctity of human life. Our Declaration of Independence said it's a creator who endowed us with inalienable rights given to us from God, not from government. And the first of those rights is life. And I stand for that right. I stand for the right to life. The very few cases that deal with those exceptions are the very tiniest of fraction of cases, and yet they get all the attention. Where all of the firepower is, is on the genuine issue of taking an innocent human life.

PAWLENTY: The National Review Online said based on results—not just based on words—I was probably the most pro-life candidate in this race.

Source: GOP primary debate in Manchester NH, June 13, 2011

Palin on Right to Life

Choose life even in case of rape or teenage pregnancy

There's no better training ground for politics than motherhood. At one point during the 2006 general election, motherhood became the focus of a unique line of questioning. In my responses to a series of debate questions on abortion, I remained consistent and sincere, explaining how personal and sensitive the issue is and that good people can disagree.

But the debate moderator decided to personalize his hypotheticals with a series of "what if..." questions:

Q: If a woman were, say, raped...

A: I would choose life.

Q: If your daughter were pregnant...

A: Again, I would choose life."

Q: If your teenage daughter got pregnant...

A: I'd counsel a young parent to choose life & consider adoption.

I calmly repeated my answers to all of his "what-ifs," then looked pointedly to my right and my left, to one opponent, then the other. Then I returned to the moderator and said, "I'm confident you'll be asking the other candidates these same questions, right?" Of course, he didn't.

Source: Going Rogue, by Sarah Palin, p.115-116, Nov. 17, 2009

Bachmann on Constitutionality of Abortion

Supreme Court justified abortion out of thin air

Our state senator proposed to install a bust o former Supreme Court justice Harry Blackmun at the state capitol; Blackmun was a famous Minnesotan, to be sure, but he was particularly beloved by liberals because he had authored the Supreme Court's infamous 1973 Roe v. Wade decision, trampling state laws and legalizing abortion nationwide. And that was an unprecedented decree lacking constitutional substance.

Blackmun absurdly declared that the basis for the Roe v. Wade decision could be found in the "penumbras" or shadows of the Constitution. In other words, Blackmun's justification for legalizing abortion was made out of thin air.

Source: Core of Conviction, by Michele Bachmann, pp. 3-4, Nov. 21, 2011

NOTE: The essence of the 1973 Roe v. Wade decision is that Constitutional rights apply only after birth; hence abortion does not breach a person's right to life. States cannot regulate 1st trimester abortions; states can regulate but not ban 2nd trimester abortions; and states can ban 3rd trimester abortions (as many have).

Palin on Constitutionality of Abortion

Constitution does offer an inherent right to privacy

Q: Do you think there's an inherent right to privacy in the Constitution?

A: I do. Yeah, I do.

Q: The cornerstone of Roe v. Wade.

A: I do. And I believe that individual states can best handle what the people within the different constituencies in the 50 states would like to see their will ushered in an issue like that.

Source: CBS News presidential interview with Katie Couric, Oct. 1, 2008

Abortion should be states' issue, not federal mandate

Q: Why is Roe v. Wade a bad decision?

A: I think it should be a states' issue not a federal government-mandated, mandating yes or no on such an important issue. I'm, in that sense, a federalist, where I believe that states should have more say in the laws of their lands and individual areas. Now, foundationally, it's no secret that I'm pro-life that I believe in a culture of life is very important for this country. Personally that's what I would like to see further embraced by America.

Source: CBS News presidential interview with Katie Couric, Oct. 1, 2008

Bachmann on Adoption

Leading advocate for foster and adopted children

Michele and Marcus have five children, Lucas, Harrison, Elisa, Caroline, and Sophia. In addition, the Bachmann family has opened their home to 23 foster children, which has inspired Michele to become one of Congress' leading advocates for foster and adopted children, earning her bipartisan praise for her efforts.

Source: Campaign website, michelebachmann.com, "About," Dec. 22, 2011

Palin on Adoption

Adoption is best plan for permanency for foster care kids

WHEREAS, there is nothing more important to Alaska than the safe growth, development, and nurturance of Alaska's children. It is our children who will determine the direction of Alaska in future years.

WHEREAS, Alaska has 847 children living in out-of-home care who cannot return to their birth parents and need the security, encouragement, safety, and cultural continuity that a permanent family can provide.

WHEREAS, adoption is the plan for permanency for these children. In 2006, 226 children from foster care achieved finalized adoption with families in Alaska.

WHEREAS, children waiting for adoptive parents and adoptive families require and deserve community and agency support.

NOW, THEREFORE, I, Sarah Palin, Governor of the State of Alaska, do hereby proclaim November 2007 as Adoption Awareness Month in Alaska, and encourage all Alaskans to become involved in community and state efforts to provide all our children with secure, nurturing, permanent families.

Source: Alaska Governor's Office: Proclamation, "Adoption," Oct. 22, 2007

Bachmann on Feminism

Fight the faddish fog of feminism

[In the 1980s] I had to see through the faddish fog of "feminism," the radical school of thought propounded by such well-known figures as Betty Friedan and Gloria Steinem. I'm all for strong women as role models. Yet in the 70s, women were solemnly instructed by the liberal media to believe that family, tradition, and even faith were merely the disguised manifestations of an oppressive "patriarchy." We were further told that "women" wanted to be liberated—as if "women" were a bloc, and as if liberals knew what was good for all of us, all across the country.

I rejected that kind of feminism. I was repulsed by the generalized worldview of liberal-left feminism, which tended to say things like, "A woman needs a man like a fish needs a bicycle." It's a free country, of course, and everyone is entitled to his or her opinion, but I wanted no part of an ideology that praised wives being apart from husbands of children being apart from fathers.

Source: Core of Conviction, by Michele Bachmann, p. 76-77, Nov. 21, 2011

Palin on Feminism

New feminism: pro-woman, pro-life sisterhood

Together, the pro-woman, pro-life sisterhood is telling the young women of America that they are capable of handling an unintended pregnancy and still pursue a career and an education. Strangely, many feminists seem to want to tell these young women that they're *not* capable, that you *can't* give your child life and still pursue your dreams. The message is: "Women, you are not strong enough or smart enough to do both. You are not capable."

The *new* feminism is telling women they are capable and strong. And if keeping a child isn't possible, adoption is a beautiful choice. It's about empowering women to make *real choices*, not forcing them to accept false ones. It's about compassion and letting these scared young women know that there will be some help there for them to raise their children in those less-than-ideal circumstances.

I believe this so strongly because I've been there. I never planned on being the mother of a son with special needs. I thought, "God will never give me something I can't handle."

Source: America by Heart, by Sarah Palin, p.153, Nov. 23, 2010

Bachmann on Definition of Marriage

I support federal *and* state marriage amendments

SANTORUM: [to Bachmann]: We can't have 50 marriage laws. This was the approach that the left took on abortion, which is to pick a few states, and then go to the Supreme Court and say "equal protection," then you will have at the Supreme Court deciding what marriage is in this country. You have to fight in each state. And there's where I disagree with Rick Perry, I disagree with Michele Bachmann. I will come to the states and fight to make sure this strategy of picking off a state here and there does not be successful in transforming marriage.

BACHMANN: I support the federal marriage amendment, because I believe that we will see this issue at the Supreme Court someday. And as president, I will not nominate activist judges who legislate from the bench. I also want to say, when I was in Minnesota, I was the chief author of the constitutional amendment to define marriage as one man, one woman. I have an absolutely unblemished record when it comes to this issue of man-woman marriage.

Source: Iowa Straw Poll GOP debate in Ames Iowa, Aug. 11, 2011

Palin on Definition of Marriage

Non-support of anything but traditional marriage

Q: Do you support, as they do in Alaska, granting same-sex benefits to couples?

BIDEN: Absolutely positively. Absolutely no distinction from a legal standpoint between a same-sex and a heterosexual couple. That's only fair.

Q: Would you support expanding that beyond Alaska to the rest of the nation?

PALIN: Well, not if it goes closer and closer towards redefining the traditional definition of marriage between one man and one woman. And unfortunately that's sometimes where those steps lead. I don't support defining marriage as anything but between one man and one woman, and I think through nuances we can go round and round about what that actually means. I'm being as straight up with Americans as I can in my non- support for anything but a traditional definition of marriage.

Q: Let's try to avoid nuance. Do you support gay marriage?

BIDEN: No. We do not support that. That is a decision to be able to be left to faiths.

PALIN: My answer is the same as his and it is that I do not.

Source: Vice Presidential debate against Sen. Joe Biden, Oct. 2, 2008

Bachmann on Gay Job Rights

NO on prohibiting job discrimination
based on sexual orientation

HR3685: Employment Non-Discrimination Act: Makes it an unlawful employment practice to discriminate against an individual on the basis of actual or perceived sexual orientation, including actions based on the actual or perceived sexual orientation of a person with whom the individual associates or has associated.

Proponents support voting YES because: Rep. CASTOR: The march towards equality under the law for all of our citizens has sometimes been slow, but it has been steady. Over time, Congress has outlawed discrimination in the workplace, based upon a person's race, gender, age, national origin, religion and disability, because when it comes to employment, these decisions are rightly based upon a person's qualifications and job performance. This legislation that outlaws job discrimination based upon sexual orientation was first introduced over 30 years ago.

Opponents recommend voting NO because: Rep. HASTINGS: Federal law bans job discrimination based on race, color, national origin, or gender. I strongly oppose discrimination in the workplace. However, I do not think it is the place of the Federal Government to legislate how each and every workplace operates. A number of States have enacted State laws prohibiting discrimination on the basis of sexual orientation. That is their right. Many businesses have chosen to adopt their own policies. That is appropriate as well. This bill as written would expand Federal law into a realm where *perception* would be a measure under discrimination law.

Source: Employment Non-Discrimination Act; HR3685 ; vote 1057, Nov. 13, 2007

Palin on Gay Job Rights

Ok to deny benefits to homosexual couples

Here's what Sarah Palin has to say about same-sex marriage. Palin said she's not out to judge anyone and has good friends who are gay, but that she supported the 1998 constitutional amendment.

Elected officials can't defy the court when it comes to how rights are applied, she said, but she would support a ballot question that would deny benefits to homosexual couples. "I believe that honoring the family structure is that important," Palin said. She said she doesn't know if people choose to be gay.

Source: Anchorage Daily News, "Little play," by K. Hopkins, Aug. 6, 2006

No spousal benefits for same-sex couples

Q: Do you support the Alaska Supreme Court's ruling that spousal benefits for state employees should be given to same-sex couples?

A: No, I believe spousal benefits are reserved for married citizens as defined in our constitution.

Source: Eagle Forum 2006 Gubernatorial Candidate Questionnaire, July 31, 2006

Bachmann on School Vouchers

Voted YES on reauthorizing the
DC opportunity scholarship program

Congressional Summary: The SOAR Act award five-year grants on a competitive basis to nonprofit organizations to carry out an expanded school choice opportunities to students who are District of Columbia residents and who come from households:

- receiving assistance under the supplemental nutrition assistance program; or

- with incomes not exceeding 185% of the poverty line.

Proponent's Argument for voting Yes: [Rep. Bishop, R-UT]: In 1996, Congress insisted upon a charter school program in DC. There is a waiting list in DC for those charter schools. In 2003, an Opportunity Scholarship was instituted. Again, there was a waiting list of people; disadvantaged kids who wanted the opportunity that this scholarship afforded them. This bill remedies both.

Opponent's Argument for voting No: [Rep. Hastings, D-FL]: In the last 41 years voters have rejected private school vouchers every time they have been proposed. In 1981, 89% of the people in a referendum in DC voted against vouchers. So how dare we come here to tell these people that we are going to thrust upon them something they don't want without a single public official in this community being consulted. Congress' oversight of the District is not an excuse for political pandering to the Republicans' special interest of the day du jour.

Source: Scholarships for Opportunity and Results Act (SOAR); H.Res186 ;
vote number 200, March 30, 2011

Palin on School Vouchers

Support charters & home schools;
not private school vouchers

Q: Would you support amending the state constitution to allow private school vouchers?

A: My priorities are to support options for education as allowable within the current funding formula—including home schools, charter schools and vocational training. This doesn't require amending the constitution.

Source: Anchorage Daily News; 2006 gubernatorial candidate profile,
Oct 22, 2006

Parents know best, about school spending & school age

Q: Do you support parental choice in the spending of state educational dollars?

A: Within Alaska law, I support parents deciding what is the best education venue for their child.

Q: Will you support efforts to raise or lower the mandatory age of education? Why or why not?

A: No, again, parents know better than government what is best for their children.

Source: Eagle Forum 2006 Gubernatorial Candidate Questionnaire, July 31, 2006

Bachmann on Education Funding

Mother of all repeal bills
for federal Department of Education

Q: What as president would you seriously do about a massive overreach of big government into the classroom?

BACHMANN: We need that to do with education what has always worked historically, and that's local control with parents. What doesn't work is what we see happen right now. I'm a mom five biological kids. We've raised 23 foster children in our home. The reason why I got involved in politics was because of the concern I had about our foster children and the education they were getting. What I would do as president of the United States is pass the mother of all repeal bills on education. I would take the entire federal education law, repeal it. Then I would go over to the Department of Education, I'd turn off the lights, I would lock the door and I would send all the money back to the states and localities.

Source: GOP Google debate in Orlando FL, Sept. 22, 2011

Palin on Education Funding

Forward Funding:
let districts plan based on advance budget

My budget priorities weren't all about slashing. We increased education funding and committed to a billion dollars into "forward funding" education so that local school districts could know how much they could count on every year. We also increased school services for children with special needs and beefed up funding for public safety officers in rural villages. But even with increased funding, I had made the largest veto totals in the state's history. It wasn't the easy path, but it was the right path.

Source: Going Rogue, by Sarah Palin, p.151, Nov. 17, 2009

Bachmann on Charter Schools

Founded New Heights Charter School: rigorous, not religious

In 1993, Marcus and I joined with other motivated neighbors to open the New Heights Charter School; immediately, some 200 students signed up. I served on the board of directors. Our goal was simple: We wanted the best possible education for children in the area, based on sound and proven principles. We wanted rigor. We wanted our kids to gain knowledge, facts, and information. We also wanted a special emphasis on help for kids with troubled backgrounds—and that was a lot of kids, even out in the leafy suburbs.

Unfortunately, within months, we were confronting dissidents and protesters who accused us of trying to advance Christian values in the schools. Yes, we were Christians, but we never sought to impose Christianity on our students. However, some liberal activists seemed to think that the word "rigorous" was somehow code for "religious."

Ultimately, I and other board members stepped down. The school survived, and today, the focus on "at risk kids" remains.

Source: Core of Conviction, by Michele Bachmann, p.114–115, Nov. 21, 2011

Palin on Charter Schools

Supports charter schools, home schools, & other alternatives

My administration will support existing programs that already offer alternative school options available throughout the state, including charter schools, rural boarding schools, home school options, correspondence schools, and vocational/technical, and magnet schools. There are many successes out there that we can look to as models. My administration will support and expand existing programs that successfully offer new approaches to ensure an appropriate education for every child in Alaska.

Source: Palin-Parnell campaign booklet: New Energy for Alaska, Nov. 3, 2006

Bachmann on Evolution

Don't censor intelligent design, but it's a state issue

While emphasizing that she didn't have a platform position on teaching evolution—since she believed it wasn't something the federal government and president should be involved in—Bachmann said her religious beliefs informed her scientific views and that sufficient questions have been raised concerning evolution to justify alternative theories to be discussed in science classes.

"I do believe that God created the earth and I believe that there are issues that need to be addressed—the Second Law of Thermodynamics, the issue of irreducible complexity, the dearth of fossil record," she said. "Those are all very real issues that should be addressed in science classes."

Not allowing ideas like intelligent design to be discussed in science classes amounted to government censorship, she said. "I think the one thing we do not want to have is censorship by government," she said. "Government shouldn't be dictating what information goes on the table."

Source: Jason Noble in Des Moines Register, "Early Life in Iowa," Nov. 30, 2011

Palin on Evolution

Supports microevolution,
but not that humans came from fish

In an Aug. 2008 vetting session, the conversation turned to the topic of theories of origins. I believed in the evidence for microevolution—that species change occurs incrementally over time. But I didn't believe in the theory that human beings originated from fish that sprouted legs. I believed we came about through a random process, but were created by God.

"But your dad's a science teacher," McCain's adviser objected.

"Yes."

"Then you know that science proves evolution."

"Parts of evolution," I said. "But I believe that God created us and also that He can create an evolutionary process that allows species to adapt."

The adviser winced. I had just dared to mention the C-word : creationism. But I felt I was on solid factual ground. Never had Dad or anyone else convinced me that the earth had sprung forth conveniently stocked with the ingredients necessary to spontaneously generate life; in fact, I thought that idea flew in the face of the evidence I saw all around.

Source: Going Rogue, by Sarah Palin, p.217-218, Nov. 17, 2009

Bachmann on No Child Left Behind

No Child Left Behind imposes 50 new state mandates

I will admit I was disappointed to see President Bush push through the No Child Left Behind Act, which the president signed into law in early 2002. No Child Left Behind was an updated Goals 2000, imposing new mandates on all 50 states—the same federal government good intentions leading to the same downward educational results. We made progress toward the repeal of the Profile of Learning in our state, and yet in the US as a whole, we were handing local classrooms over to the federal bureaucracy.

Source: Core of Conviction, by Michele Bachmann, p.127, Nov. 21, 2011

NOTE: NCLB is the 2001 bipartisan law intended to improve K-12 schools, under the theory of standards-based education reform. States are required to establish standardized testing, so that all high school graduates meet the test criteria. States are also required to give options (school choice) to students who attend schools that fail to meet NCLB's standards. The controversy over NCLB currently focuses on funding: Opponents of NCLB argue that states are provided inadequate federal funding for implementation of NCLB, and that therefore NCLB represents an "unfunded mandate" on states.

Palin on No Child Left Behind

294 Alaska public schools progressed under NCLB

Congratulations to the staff at the 294 Alaska public schools that made adequate yearly progress under the federal No Child Left Behind (NCLB) standards for the 2007-2008 school year. Our schools faced a higher bar in 2007-2008 for the percentages of students who score proficient in language arts and math assessments. Congratulations to the many schools that continue to improve in student achievement but may have fallen short in 1 or 2 of the 31 categories schools are held accountable for in NCLB.

Source: Alaska Governor's Office: August 2008 Newsletter, Aug. 20, 2008

We need more flexibility in No Child Left Behind

America needs to be putting a lot more focus on education and our schools have got to be really ramped up in terms of the funding that they are deserving. Teachers needed to be paid more. I come from a house full of school teachers. We have got to increase the standards. No Child Left Behind was implemented. It's not doing the job though. We need flexibility in No Child Left Behind. We need to put more of an emphasis on the profession of teaching. My kids as public school participants right now, it's near and dear to my heart.

Source: Vice Presidential debate against Joe Biden, Oct. 2, 2008

Bachmann on Traditional Families

Support traditional family life

My record of supporting traditional marriage, family life and children, including those yet born, is unambiguous. This will not change if elected to Congress.

Source: 2006 House campaign website, michelebachmann.com, "Issues," Nov 7, 2006

Best results when family involved; worst with government

Q: Your comment on Gov. Perry trying to forcibly vaccinate 12-year-old girls against sexually transmitted diseases?

BACHMANN: Well, what I'm very concerned about is the issue of parental rights. I think when it comes to dealing with children, it's the parents who need to make that decision. It is wrong for government, whether it's state or federal government, to impose on parents what they must do to inoculate their children. This is very serious, and I think that it's very important that parents have the right. We have the best results when we have the private sector and when we have the family involved. We have the worst results when the federal government gets involved, and especially by dictate to impose something like an inoculation on an innocent 12-year-old girl. I would certainly oppose that.

Source: GOP debate in Simi Valley CA at the Reagan Library, Sept. 7, 2011

Palin on Traditional Families

Founding Fathers took strong families for granted

It sounds strange to us today, given how preoccupied we can be with the problems the family faces, that the men who laid the foundation of our republic said so little about the institution of the family. The founders took it for granted that strong families instilled in children the habits and disciplines necessary for those children to govern themselves in adulthood.

What the founders focused their energy on, then, wasn't a government that sought to control or shape families, but a government that could capitalize on the virtues of trust and self-restraint that families create—a government that could respect and honor good citizens by allowing them to liver and prosper in freedom. The Constitution's relationship to the family, then, was meant to be reciprocal: to depend upon the virtues of family life to make its system of government work, while protecting the freedom of families to create self-governing citizens.

Source: America by Heart, by Sarah Palin, p.111-112, Nov. 23, 2010

Bachmann on Welfare Reform

Government subsidizes idleness, dependency, and delinquency

In our efforts to protect the family, I began to see that our government was often on the wrong side. Government officials were praising, even subsidizing, the worst kinds of behavior—not just abortion but also idleness, dependency, and delinquency. The pundits of [the 1970s and 1980s] called it "justice" and "liberation." But here on the ground, in real-world America, where I was living, the rest of us could see that government was fostering injustice and anarchy.

Indeed, in the seventies the bad trends were moving steadily up and the bad trends were moving down: abortion, crime, divorce, drug abuse, and venereal disease were on the rise, while test scores, the purchasing power of the dollar, and traditional family values were drastically falling.

Good moral behavior, I realized, is not just the path to a virtuous civil society; it is the prerequisite for economic growth. A healthy society; a healthy economy.

Source: Core of Conviction, by Michele Bachmann, p. 48, Nov. 21, 2011

Palin on Welfare Reform

EITC moves thousands
of welfare recipients into workforce

WHEREAS, the Earned Income Tax Credit (EITC) is a refundable federal income tax credit for people who work but earn low wages. It is a work-support program, designed to encourage work by providing a financial incentive to work and by allowing low-income workers to keep more of the money they earn.

WHEREAS, the EITC has encouraged hundreds of thousands of welfare recipients to enter the workforce; it continues to lift more families out of poverty than any other federal program;

WHEREAS, the EITC put roughly $60 million into the pockets of Alaska's low-income working families and individuals last year.

WHEREAS, unfortunately, each year many qualified people fail to apply for the EITC because they do not know about it, do not know they are eligible, or do not know how to apply.

NOW, THEREFORE, I, Gov. Sarah Palin, do hereby proclaim Feb. 1, 2008, as Alaska Earned Income Tax Credit Awareness Day, and urge Alaskans who are eligible to apply for the EITC.

Source: Alaska Governor's Office: Proclamation, "EITC Awareness," Jan. 31, 2008

Bachmann on Democratic Party

Switched party in 1970s; Democratic Party left us

In 1980, I became a Republican and never looked back. [After voting for Jimmy Carter in 1976], I realized I wasn't in line with the new anti-family, anti-strong defense, anti-fiscal sanity Democratic Party. I was now a Republican.

As Ronald Reagan always liked to say, he didn't leave the Democratic Party—the Democratic Party left him. Now I too knew the feeling.

Indeed, during the late seventies, Marcus and I grew increasingly attracted to Reagan and his conservative philosophy. We loved it when he said that Americans wanted a conservatism of bright colors, not pale pastels—we sure did. That is, we wanted someone who would unabashedly take the fight directly to the economic declinists, the foreign policy defeatists, and the anti-family relativists who seemed at the time to dominate both parties. Republicans of the "me-too" persuasion held no appeal to us. We wanted a GOP that would fight to make real change. So we liked Reagan.

Source: Core of Conviction, by Michele Bachmann, p. 73, Nov. 21, 2011

Palin on Democratic Party

OpEd: Darling of the Democrats
for taking on GOP incumbent

[An Alaska resident writes in an epilogue entitled "A View From Alaska"]:

Democrats forget when Palin was the Darling of the Democrats, because as soon as Palin took the governor's office away from a fellow Republican and tough SOB, Frank Murkowski, she tore into the Republican's "Corrupt Bastards Club" (CBC) and sent it packing, [oome to jail]. The Democrats reacted by skipping around the yard and throwing confetti. Name another governor in this country who has ever done anything similar.

Source: Going Rogue, by Sarah Palin, p.405-406, Nov. 17, 2009

Bachmann on the Tea Party

Tea Party has held Congress to account

Q: What role will the Tea Party play in the 2012 elections?

A: As chair of the House Tea Party Caucus, I know how positive an influence the Tea Party has been. They've held Congress to account. Despite media misrepresentations the Tea Party represents all Americans; disaffected Democrats, independents, libertarians, and the GOP. The Tea Party will lead the fight to restore limited government, repeal Obamacare, lower spending & cut taxes.

Source: Republican primary debate on Twitter.com, July 21, 2011

Chairs the House Tea Party Caucus

Q: Does the Tea Party push out mainstream Republicans?

A: I'm the chairman of the Tea Party Caucus in the House of Representatives. And what I've seen is unlike how the media has tried to wrongly and grossly portray the Tea Party, the Tea Party is really made up of disaffected Democrats, independents, people who've never been political a day in their life. People who are libertarians, or Republicans. It's a wide swath of America coming together. I think that's why the left fears it so much. Because they're people who simply want to take the country back. They want the country to work again.

Source: GOP primary debate in Manchester NH, June 13, 2011

Palin on the Tea Party

Tea Partiers love America
and dislike what's happening to her

What I've learned from the Tea Party Express is this: the spark of patriotic indignation that inspired the Americans who fought for our freedom and independence has been ignited once again! They've seen what is happening in America, so they've decided to get involved. They feel like they're losing something good and fundamental about their country, so they've decided to take it back, because they love this country and are proud to be Americans!

I realized that the Tea Partiers are normal Americans who haven't necessarily been involved in national politics before but are turned on to this movement because they love America and they don't like what they see happening to her. They're so concerned about the path we're on that they've decided to get involved.

Source: America by Heart, by Sarah Palin, p. xii–xiii, Nov. 23, 2010

Republican Party should absorb Tea Party movement

Q: How do you see the future of the Tea Party movement? As part of the Republican Party or a third independent party?

A: The Republican Party would be really smart to start trying to absorb as much of the Tea Party movement as possible because this is the future of our country. The Tea Party movement is the future of politics because it is shaping the way politics are conducted. You've got really both party machines running scared.

Source: Tea Party Convention Q&A, Feb. 6, 2010

Bachmann vs. Palin on International Issues

International issues focus on foreign relations and anything involving foreign nations, including the following topics:

- *Energy and Oil:* including global warming, domestic drilling and alternative energy sources. The two politicians agree on domestic drilling and opposing cap-and-trade.

- *Free Trade:* including NAFTA (the North American Free Trade Agreement) and other bilateral agreements. Bachmann and Palin agree on free trade with restrictions.

- *Immigration:* including border security; the border fence; and dealing with the current 12 million illegal immigrants in the US. Bachmann takes a hard line against immigrants; Palin is more moderate on this issue.

- *Foreign Policy:* Bachmann and Palin both support "American Exceptionalism." Bachmann is well-established as a foreign policy expert based on her service in the House Intelligence committee; Palin has been studying since her early 2008 foreign policy flubs.

- *Homeland Security:* this category concerns defense policy, not war policy. This category includes defense spending issues; and defense strategy goals. Bachmann and Palin agree on defense increases, and on tough talk on terrorism.

- *War and Peace:* including the current ongoing wars in Iraq and Afghanistan. Palin and Bachmann agree on maintaining a US military presence in both countries.

Bachmann on International Issues

Palin on
International Issues

Bachmann on Cap-and-Trade

I opposed cap-and-trade, including Lightbulb Choice Act

Q: There's an expression "Minnesota Nice." And some people believe that both of you have tested it in recent weeks. Gov. Pawlenty said you have no accomplishments in Congress?

BACHMANN: When you were governor in Minnesota you implemented cap and trade in our state and you praised the unconstitutional individual mandates and called for requiring all people in our state to purchase health insurance. You said the era of small government was over. That sounds more like Barack Obama, if you ask me. During my time in the US Congress I have fought all of these unconstitutional measures. The policies that the governor advocated for were cap and trade. When it came to cap and trade, I fought it with everything that was in me, including introducing the Lightbulb Freedom of Choice Act so people could all purchase the lightbulb of their choice.

Source: Iowa Straw Poll GOP debate in Ames Iowa, Aug. 11, 2011

NOTE: "Cap-and-Trade" refers to a proposed greenhouse gas reduction program. The "cap" refers to a government-specified limit on total greenhouse gas emissions. Then companies would "trade" greenhouse gas emission permits at a price determined by the free market. The result would be instituting a new fee for emitting carbon dioxide and other greenhouse gases.

Palin on Cap-and-Trade

Cap-and-Trade is a Cap-and-Tax program

We can't abandon free-market principles in order to save the free market. The cure only makes the disease worse.

One such cure: Washington's misguided "Cap and Trade plan. But let's call it what it is: a Cap and Tax program. The environmentalists' plan to reduce pollution is to tax businesses according to how much pollution they produce. Businesses that reduce emissions could trade or sell their government credits to other companies.

We'll all feel the effects of this misguided plan to buy and sell pollution. The president has already admitted that the policy he seeks will cause our electricity bills to "skyrocket." Sadly, those hit hardest will be those who are already struggling to make ends meet. So much for the campaign promise not to raise taxes on anyone making less than $250,000 a year. This is a tax on everyone.

As more and more Americans understand that cap and trade is an environmentalist Ponzi scheme in which only the government benefits, they will refuse to tolerate it.

Source: Going Rogue, by Sarah Palin, p.390-391, Nov. 17, 2009

Bachmann on Drilling Policy

Tap the natural abundance of Alaska and the lower 48

Back in the 70s, I remember being appalled by Carter's energy policy; he was telling us to turn the thermostat down & build giant "synfuel" plants. These proposals struck me as either unnecessary sacrifice or an unnecessary boondoggle. After all, I had seen for myself the natural abundance of Alaska—although little did I know, as yet, about the untapped energy supplies abounding in the lower 48, both underground and offshore.

Meanwhile, as day follows night, Carter's bad policies were leading to bad results. America was suffering from a severe gasoline shortage, all the worse because it was government created. I remember sitting in a gas line for more than an hour, only to see the station owner put up a "no gas" sign right in front of me—he had run out. The bureaucrats simply weren't allowing him enough gas.

Source: Core of Conviction, by Michele Bachmann, p. 65, Nov. 21, 2011

Voted YES on opening
Outer Continental Shelf to oil drilling

Congressional Summary: Makes available for leasing, in the 2012-2017 five-year oil and gas leasing program, outer Continental Shelf areas that are estimated to contain more than 2.5 billion barrels of oil; or are estimated to contain more than 7.5 trillion cubic feet of natural gas.

Source: Reversing Pres. Obama's Offshore Moratorium Act;
Bill H.1231 ; vote number 320 on May 12, 2011

Palin on Drilling Policy

Drill, baby, drill

BIDEN: We have 3% of the world's oil reserves. We consume 25% of the oil. John has voted 20 times in the last decade-and-a-half against funding alternative energy sources, clean energy sources, wind, solar, biofuels. McCain thinks, I guess, the only answer is drill, drill, drill. Drill we must, but it'll take ten years before any [new drilling delivers oil].

PALIN: The chant is "drill, baby, drill." That's what we hear across this country in our rallies because people are hungry for those domestic sources of energy to be tapped into. They know that even in my own energy-producing state we have billions of barrels of oil and hundreds of trillions of cubic feet of clean, green natural gas. Barack Obama and Sen. Biden, you've said no to everything in trying to find a domestic solution to the energy crisis. You even called drilling—safe, environmentally-friendly drilling offshore as raping the outer continental shelf.

Source: Vice Presidential debate against Joe Biden, Oct. 2, 2008

Bachmann on Free Trade

Free and fair trade agreements spur economic growth

Each day in Minnesota and all across the nation, billions of dollars' worth of products begin their journey to be sold overseas. American farmers, manufacturers, and businesses rely on exports to strengthen and grow both their bottom line, as well as our economy's.

Free and fair trade agreements help spur economic growth; improve efficiency and innovation; create better, higher-paying jobs for hard-working Americans; and increase the availability of lower-priced products here in the United States.

Furthermore, the role of free trade as an expression of liberty and opportunity for all individuals signifies the very principles our country was founded upon. Yet, the free trade agreements with Panama, South Korea and Colombia negotiated under the Bush Administration remain little more than words on paper. Despite having been carefully negotiated over a period of two and half years, these agreements have become bogged down by partisan divides.

Source: Michele Bachmann column on Heritage Foundation website, Oct. 16, 2009

Palin on Free Trade

Trade important to Alaska,
but keep Alaska residents first

Alaskans have been first-rate at international trade for decades. To our friends in international markets, thank you for your friendship and trade. Alaska welcomes your business and investment.

International trade is important to Alaska. Our exports grew more than 12% last year, and, for the first time, our annual exports topped $4 billion in 2006. We are helping our economy and economies around the world through trade.

In all our efforts, we will keep Alaska residents first. We will help Alaska businesses succeed in their key international markets. We will improve Alaska's positive international relations with our key trading partners. We will help open new doors.

Education helps trade, too. International courses at our schools and universities help us excel in international markets. We must further prepare Alaskans for international investment and trade opportunities by encouraging education that includes strong workforce development for our high-wage energy and mining industries.

Source: Letter from the governor on state trade website, Sept. 1, 2008

Bachmann on Illegal Immigration

It's not the American way to give immigrants' rights

Sen. SANTORUM: What Gov. Perry's done is he provided in-state tuition for illegal immigrants.

Gov. PERRY: If you're pursuing citizenship, you pay in-state tuition. It doesn't make any difference what the sound of your last name is. That is the American way.

Q [to Bachmann]: Is that basically Obama's DREAM Act?

BACHMANN: Yes, it's very similar. And I think that the American way is not to give taxpayer subsidized benefits to people who have broken our laws or who are here in the US illegally. That is not the American way. Because the immigration system worked very well up until the mid-1960s when liberal members of Congress changed the immigration laws. What works is to have people come into the US with a little bit of money in their pocket legally with sponsors so that if anything happens to them, they don't fall back on the taxpayers to take care of them. And then they also have to agree to learn the speak the English language, learn American history and our constitution. That's the American way.

Source: GOP Tea Party debate in Tampa FL, Sept. 12, 2011

Palin on Illegal Immigration

Supports a path to citizenship,
but no amnesty for illegals

Q: Should undocumented immigrants all be deported?

A: There is no way that in the US we would roundup every illegal immigrant—there are about 12 million of the illegal immigrants—not only economically is that just an impossibility but that's not a humane way anyway to deal with the issue.

Q: Do you then favor an amnesty for the 12 million undocumented immigrants?

A: No, I do not. Not total amnesty. You know, people have got to follow the rules. We have got to make sure that there is equal opportunity and those who are here legally should be first in line for services being provided and those opportunities that this great country provides.

Q: So you support a path to citizenship for undocumented immigrants?

A: I do because I understand why people would want to be in America. To seek the safety and prosperity, the opportunities, the health that is here. It is so important that yes, people follow the rules so that people can be treated equally and fairly in this country.

Source: Univision Interview with Sarah Palin, by Jorge Ramos, Oct. 26, 2008

Bachmann on American Exceptionalism

American exceptionalism:
indispensable nation of the world

We need to start making things again in this country, and we can do that by reducing the tax and regulatory burdens on job creators. America will have the highest corporate tax rate in the world. Think about that. Look no further to see why jobs are moving overseas.

I believe that we are in the early days of a history-making turn in America. Congress is responding [to Tea Party voters] and we are just starting to undo the damage that's been done the last few years. Because we believe in lower taxes. We believe in a limited view of government, and exceptionalism in America. And I believe that America is the indispensable nation of the world. Just the creation of this nation itself was a miracle. Who's to say that we can't see a miracle again?

We will push forward. We will proclaim liberty throughout the land. And we will do so because we the people will never give up on this great nation.

Source: State of the Union Tea Party response, Jan. 26, 2011

Palin on American Exceptionalism

American exceptionalism based on idea of right to be free

In my experience, Americans are patriotic but not necessarily idealistic. We find inspiration and motivation close to home, in our families, our communities, and our faith. Generally, we're happy to live our lives and pursue our dreams and leave others to live and pursue theirs.

And if we were an ordinary country—just one country among many others—that would be enough. All countries have the right to defend themselves, and they exercise that right whenever necessary. But America isn't just another country, it's an exceptional country. We are the only country in the history of the world that was founded not on a particular territory or culture or people, but on an idea. That idea is that all human beings have a God-given right to be free. So when our young men and women sacrifice to serve in the military, they are doing much more than defending a piece of land. They are defending the idea of America itself.

Source: America by Heart, by Sarah Palin, p. 37, Nov. 23, 2010

Bachmann on Israel Policy

Don't force Israel back to indefensible 1967 borders

I will reverse the Obama administration's pressure on Israel, which seeks to force Israel back to its indefensible 1967 borders. Obama's policy threatens Israel's security, even as it encourages Israel's enemies to think that they can use terror, and the threat of terror, to extract dangerous concessions.

Source: Core of Conviction, by Michele Bachmann, p.198, Nov. 21, 2011

Commitment to unbreakable U.S.-Israel bond

Bachmann signed a letter to the Secretary of State:

We are writing to reaffirm our commitment to the unbreakable bond that exists between our country and the State of Israel and to express to you our deep concern over recent tension. In every important relationship, there will be occasional misunderstandings and conflicts.

Our valuable bilateral relationship with Israel needs and deserves constant reinforcement. We recognize that, despite the extraordinary closeness between our country and Israel, there will be differences over issues both large and small. Our view is that such differences are best resolved quietly, in trust and confidence, as befits longstanding strategic allies. We hope that, with mutual effort and good faith, the US and Israel will move beyond this disruption quickly, to the lasting benefit of both nations.

Source: Hoyer-Cantor letter to Clinton from 327 House members, Mar. 25, 2010

Palin on Israel Policy

Two-state solution for Israel/Palestine is a top priority

Q: How would you solve Israel/Palestinian conflict?

PALIN: A two-state solution is the solution. That needs to be done, and that will be a top agenda item under a McCain-Palin administration. Israel is our strongest and best ally in the Middle East.

BIDEN: No one in the Senate has been a better friend to Israel than Joe Biden. I would have never joined this ticket were I not absolutely sure Barack Obama shared my passion. [The Bush] administration's policy has been a failure. Bush insisted on elections on the West Bank, when I said, "Big mistake. Hamas will win." What happened? Hamas won. We kicked Hezbollah out of Lebanon, I said, "Move NATO forces in there. Fill the vacuum, because if you don't, Hezbollah will control it." Now what happened? Hezbollah is a legitimate part of the government. We will change this policy with diplomacy that understands that you must let Israel negotiate and stand with them, not insist on policies like this administration has.

Source: Vice Presidential debate against Joe Biden, Oct. 2, 2008

Bachmann on China Policy

China is building 3,000 miles of tunnels for nukes

Q: How do you open the markets in China for American companies?

BACHMANN: Well, the Chinese have been bad actors. Recently we found out that they dumped counterfeit computer chips here in the US. We're using some of those counterfeit computer chips in the Pentagon in some of our weapons systems. This has national security implications.

We also found out that the Chinese just finished building 3,000 miles of underground tunnels where they are housing some nuclear weapons. There's some very real consequences to the US overspending to such an extent that we're in hock to them over a trillion dollars.

We've sent so much interest money over to the Chinese to pay our debts off that we effectively built their aircraft carrier. And by 2015, we will be sending so much interest money over, we will be paying for the entire People's Liberation Army of China. What we need to do is stop enriching China with our money. And we do that by stop borrowing from them, by stop spending money that we don't have.

Source: CNBC GOP Primary debate in Rochester MI, Nov. 9, 2011

Palin on China Policy

Bothered by China's bid to control Alaska gasline

The competitive bidding process we created with AGIA [Alaska's 1,715-mile gasline] threw open Alaska's doors to free enterprise. Suddenly, even other nations were bidding. We had anticipated Canadian interest but were surprised to receive a proposal from China. The bid, by Sinopec, bothered me. There was little doubt the company could muster the manpower, technology, and funding necessary to do the job, but this proposal skated on the razor's edge between the free market and national sovereignty. An energy-thirsty Communist nation controlling Alaska's natural gas reserves was not in the best interest of the state or our country. It turned out Sinopec's application was incomplete anyway, and was rejected for that reason.

The Calgary-based pipeline building giant TransCanada-Alaska had not only met every enforceable requirement, but exceeded them. We were ecstatic.

In Aug. 2008, we awarded the AGIA license. We had turned the idea of commercializing our natural gas from pipe dream to pipeline.

Source: Going Rogue, by Sarah Palin, p.205-207, Nov. 17, 2009

Bachmann on Pakistan Policy

Continue aid to Pakistan, but get more intel from them

PERRY: [to Bachmann]: If we want to engage [Pakistan], writing a blank check is nonsensical.

BACHMANN: With all due respect to the governor, I think that's highly naive, because, again, we have to recognize what's happening on the ground. These are nuclear weapons all across this nation. And, potentially, Al Qaida could get hold of these weapons. These weapons could find their way out of Pakistan, into New York City or into Washington, DC. That's how serious this is. We have to maintain an American presence.

PERRY: Absolutely we need to be engaged. I just said we need to quit writing blank checks to these countries, and then letting them decide how these dollars are going to be spent.

BACHMANN: We're not writing just blank checks. We're also exchanging intelligence information. So we aren't writing blank checks in that region.

Source: CNN National Security GOP primary debate, Nov. 22, 2011

Palin on Pakistan Policy

Keep option to go into Pakistan to go after terrorists

Q: Do we have the right to be making cross-border attacks into Pakistan from Afghanistan, with or without the approval of the Pakistani government?

A: We're going to work with these countries, building new relationships, working with existing allies, but forging new ones also, in order to get to a point in this world where war is not going to be a first option. In fact, war has got to be, a military strike, a last option.

Q: But do we have the right to go across the border without the approval of the Pakistan?

A: In order to stop Islamic extremists, those terrorists who would seek to destroy America & our allies, we must do whatever it takes and we must not blink in making those tough decisions of where we go and even who we target.

Q: Is that a yes? That we have the right to go across the border?

A: I believe that America has to exercise all options in order to stop the terrorists who are hell bent on destroying America and our allies. We have got to have all options out there on the table.

Source: ABC News: 2008 election interview with Charlie Gibson, Sept. 11, 2008

Bachmann on North Korea

North Korea is the
Wal-Mart of missile weapon delivery systems

Michele Bachman is taking aim at her rivals as she works to win the support of "values voters."

A member of the House Intelligence Committee, Bachmann said she is the strongest candidate on national security issues. S h e warned against expecting a change in North Korean foreign policy in the wake of Kim Jong Il's death. North Korea, a state sponsor of terror, has been the "Wal-Mart of missile weapon delivery systems," she said.

Source: IowaCaucus.com, "Authentic Voice"   *, Dec. 20, 2011*

Palin on North Korea

Economic sanctions on North Korea for nukes

Q: What should be the trigger for nuclear weapons use?

PALIN: Our nuclear weaponry here in the US is used as a deterrent. And that's a safe, stable way to use nuclear weaponry. For North Korea under Kim Jong Il, we have got to make sure that we're putting economic sanctions on these countries and that we have allies supporting us in this, to make sure that leaders like Kim Jong Il & [Iran's president] Ahmadinejad are not allowed to acquire, to proliferate, or to use those nuclear weapons. It is that important.

Source: Vice Presidential debate against Sen. Joe Biden, Oct. 2, 2008

Bachmann on Iranian Nukes

Biggest issue in Middle East is nuclear Iran

The president has not done what he needs to do to keep the US safe. If you look at the biggest issue in the Middle East, it's a nuclear Iran, and the president has taken his eyes off that prize. He's said to Israel that they need to shrink back to their indefensible 1967 borders. I sit on the House Permanent Select Committee on Intelligence. We deal with the nation's classified secrets. And I firmly believe that the president has weakened us militarily and put us more at risk than at any time.

Source: GOP debate in Simi Valley CA at the Reagan Library, Sept. 7, 2011

Palin on Iranian Nukes

Nuclear Iran is dangerous to whole world

Q: Do you consider a nuclear Iran to be an existential threat to Israel?

A: I believe that under the leadership of Ahmadinejad, nuclear weapons in the hands of his government are extremely dangerous to everyone on this globe.

Q: So what should we do about a nuclear Iran?

A: We have got to make sure that nuclear weapons are not given to those hands of Ahmadinejad, not that he would use them, but that he would allow terrorists to be able to use them. So we have got to put the pressure on Iran.

Source: ABC News: 2008 election interview with Charlie Gibson, Sept. 11, 2008

Bachmann on War on Terror

Absolute policy of not negotiating with terrorists

Q: [to Cain]: Israel has just negotiated with Palestine to exchange 1,000 Palestinian prisoners for one Israeli soldier. If al Qaeda had an American soldier in captivity, and they demanded the release of everyone at Guantanamo Bay, would you release them?

CAIN: You would have to consider the entire situation.

BACHMANN: This is a very serious issue. For any candidate to say that they would release the prisoners at Guantanamo in exchange for a hostage would be absolutely contrary to the historical nature of the US and what we do in our policy. That's naive; we cannot do that. The US has done well because we have an absolute policy: We don't negotiate.

CAIN: No, I believe in the philosophy of we don't negotiate with terrorists. I would never agree to letting hostages in Guantanamo Bay go. No, that wasn't the intent at all.

Source: GOP primary debate in Las Vegas, Oct. 18, 2011

Palin on War on Terror

Palin Plan on terrorism: We win, they lose

Q: We know the Obama plan; what's the Palin plan when it comes to the war on terror?

A: When it comes to national security, as I ratchet down the message on national security, it's easy to just kind of sum it up by repeating Ronald Reagan when he talked about the Cold War. And we can apply this now to our war on terrorism, you know. Bottom line, we win, they lose. We do all that we can to win.

Source: Tea Party Convention Q&A, Feb. 6, 2010

Bachmann on Captured Terrorists

No Miranda rights for terrorists; expand Guantanamo

Q: You say that we don't win the war on terror by closing Guantanamo and reading Miranda rights to terrorists. Rep. Paul says terrorism suspects have committed a crime and should be given due process in civilian courts. Why is he wrong?

BACHMANN: Because terrorists who commit acts against US citizens, people who are from foreign countries who do that, do not have any rights under our Constitution, nor Miranda rights. We've also seen that Guantanamo Bay has yielded significant information. In fact, we've learned that that led to the capture and the killing of bin Laden. This is a tool that we need to have in order to be able to prostitute the new type of war, the new type of warfare, and the new type of terrorists that this country is dealing with.

PAUL: She turns our rule of law on its head. I thought our courts recognized that you had to be tried. We've brought nearly 300 individuals from Pakistan and other places, given them a trial in this country, and put them in prison.

Source: Iowa Straw Poll GOP debate in Ames Iowa, Aug. 11, 2011

Palin on Captured Terrorists

Question terrorists
before they get lawyered up & Mirandized

On Christmas day, the system did not work. This terrorist trained in Yemen with al Qaeda. His American visa was not revoked until after he tried to kill hundreds of passengers.

What followed was equally disturbing after he was captured. He was questioned for only 50 minutes. We have a choice in how to do this. The choice was only question him for 50 minutes and then read his Miranda rights. The administration says then there are no downsides or upsides to treating terrorists like civilian criminal defendants. But a lot of us would beg to differ. For example, there are questions we would have liked this foreign terrorist to answer before he lawyered up and invoked our U.S. constitutional right to remain silent.

Source: Tea Party Convention speeches, Feb. 6, 2010

Focus on fighting Al-Qaeda terrorists,
not on reading rights

[Barack Obama] seeks to reduce the strength of America in a dangerous world.

Victory in Iraq is finally in sight... he wants to forfeit. Terrorist states are seeking nuclear weapons without delay... he wants to meet them without preconditions. Al-Qaida terrorists still plot to inflict catastrophic harm... he's worried that someone won't read them their rights?

Source: Speech at 2008 Republican National Convention, Sept. 3, 2008

Bachmann on Defense Spending

Defense spending did not cause our budget crisis; no cuts

Q: How do you weigh the cost of fighting the war on terror against the exploding debt crisis?

BACHMANN: I support DOD efficiency but defense spending did not cause our budget crisis & we must maintain our military strength.

CAIN: National security and protecting our borders from foreign invaders is something we as a nation really can't put a price on. Mounting deficit spending is a concern, but this spending is necessary for all Americans to enjoy our freedoms and liberties.

BACHMANN: Our security requires a strong defense and wise leadership. I will preserve our military strength while using it judiciously.

CAIN: As president, I'd support any cuts to wasteful spending in the military, but nothing more. Military is key to US safety.

BACHMANN: We must reserve military force for situations where we've been attacked, are threatened, or have vital interests at stake.

Source: Republican primary debate on Twitter.com, July 21, 2011

Palin on Defense Spending

Ask all candidates,
"Are you doing all you can for security?"

Q: Your views on national security issues?

A: I think candidates are going to be asked, are you doing—and are your intentions to do—all that you can to help secure these United States? And I think every elected official needs to ask themselves that. And I say that, even personally. My one and only son, my 18-year-old, he just signed up for the United States Army. He is at boot camp right now and I'm thinking, you know, this kid is doing all that he can within his power to help secure and defend the United States. Every elected official had better be asking themselves, are you doing as much also? Are you doing all that you can?

Source: Interview with Charlie Rose, Oct. 12, 2007

Bachmann on Iraq War

Leaving Iraq now invites in Iran as hegemon

Q: There is concern about the growing influence of Iran within Iraq. President Obama announced the final withdrawal of combat troops today. Are there any circumstances as president where you would send US troops back into Iraq?

A: The biggest mistake that President Obama has made has been the decision he made regarding Iraq. He was essentially given on a silver platter victory in Iraq, and he's choosing intentionally to lose the peace.

We all know what is going to happen. We know that Iran is going to be the hegemon and try to come into Iraq and have the dominant influence. And then Iran will essentially have dominance from the Persian Gulf all the way to the Mediterranean, through its ally Syria.

We know without a shadow of a doubt that Iran will take a nuclear weapon; they WILL use it to wipe our ally Israel off the face of the map, and they've stated they will use it against the US. Look no further than the Iranian constitution, which states unequivocally that their mission is to extend jihad across the world and eventually to set up a worldwide caliphate.

Source: Iowa caucus 2011 GOP primary debate on Fox News , *Dec. 15, 2011*

Palin on Iraq War

No white flag of surrender on Iraq

Q: What is your plan for an exit strategy?

PALIN: I am very thankful that we do have a good plan and the surge and the counterinsurgency strategy in Iraq that has proven to work, I know that the other ticket opposed this surge,

BIDEN: I didn't hear a plan. Obama offered a clear plan. Shift responsibility to Iraqis over 16 months. Draw down our combat troops. We'll end this war. For McCain, there's no end in sight.

PALIN: Your plan is a white flag of surrender in Iraq and that is not what our troops need to hear today, that's for sure. You guys opposed the surge. The surge worked. We'll know when we're finished in Iraq when the Iraqi government can govern its people and when the Iraqi security forces can secure its people. And our commanders on the ground will tell us when those conditions have been met. That victory is within sight.

Source: Vice Presidential debate against Sen. Joe Biden, Oct. 2, 2008

Retreat is defeat in Iraq

Q: Why do we need to win in Iraq?

A: Retreat is not an option. Retreat is defeat in Iraq. Al Qaeda, they're acknowledging even that Iraq is the central front on the War on Terror. If we were to lose there, we're not going to be any better off when we fight in Afghanistan either, nor the other areas where terrorist cells are.

Source: Fox News interview on "Hannity & Colmes," Sept. 17, 2008

Bachmann on Afghanistan War

Stay the course in Afghanistan

On Afghanistan, I firmly believe that we are at a point where we've got to stay the course, and we've got to finish the job. Reports coming out of Helmand right now are positive. David Petraeus is successfully prosecuting the surge.

President Bush did let the country know where we were at, and I give him a lot of credit; he stood against the world for what he knew to be right in dealing with terrorism.

Now in Afghanistan, we are making great progress. I believe that we will be victorious, and we'll end it. I understand why people are frustrated. I completely understand. But I do trust General Petraeus in that effort and in what he is doing over there. And I think that they are doing what we need to do."

Source: Matthew Continetti in The Weekly Standard, June 22, 2011

Voted NO on removing US armed forces from Afghanistan

Congressional Summary: Directs the President, pursuant to the War Powers Resolution, to remove the U.S. Armed Forces from Afghanistan, by no later than 30 days after this resolution is adopted; or if the President determines that it is not safe to remove them by such date, by no later than December 31, 2011.

Source: Resolution on Afghanistan; H.Con.Res.28 ; March 17, 2011

Palin on Afghanistan War

Surge needed in Afghanistan; we cannot afford to lose.

Q: Why support a surge in Afghanistan?

A: Because we can't afford to lose in Afghanistan, as we cannot afford to lose in Iraq, either, these central fronts on the war on terror. And I asked President Karzai, "Is that what you are seeking, also? That strategy that has worked in Iraq that John McCain had pushed for, more troops? A counterinsurgency strategy?" And he said, "yes." And he also showed great appreciation for what America and American troops are providing in his country.

Source: CBS News presidential interview with Katie Couric, Sept. 24, 2008

Book Reviews

OnTheIssues excerpts political books and debates as the primary source of the materials in this book. Following are several book reviews, plus links online to additional books and debates cited in this book.

Book reviews:

Additional book excerpts online:

Book Review:
Core of Conviction: My Story
by Rep. Michele Bachmann
(Nov 21, 2011)

This book is Bachmann's basic autobiography. It's her first autobiography, so it just covers the basics: Her family of origin; how she met her husband; how she entered politics; and an outline of her presidential campaign philosophy.

The book explores several issues that have arisen during the presidential campaign. That's unusual, since most of the presidential candidates came out with their autobiographies prior to the race, or very early in the race. Bachmann's book came out in late November 2011, after a dozen debates, and well after she had won the Iowa Straw Poll in August 2011. Hence Bachmann had the opportunity to address several of the hot issues that her opponents and the press raised:

- *Pray the Gay Away:* Bachmann's husband Marcus was accused of running, with Michele, a Christian counseling center which "cured" homosexuals. While that is partly true, Marcus is a legitimate therapist with a master's and doctor's degree in psychology. Bachmann cites their business as a counseling center with a Christian theme; the press instead portrayed it as a thinly-veiled evangelical camp.

- *Migraines:* Bachmann was accused by the press of being potentially unqualified for the presidency because she suffers from migraine headaches. Bachmann admits in this book that she does have regular migraines, for which she takes several medications. She admonishes the press for sexism, since migraines are primarily a woman's condition.

- *23 Foster Kids:* Bachmann has not released her numerous foster daughters' names (all girls; all teens) on the basis of privacy. She has been criticized for claiming that the "raised" them when she had some for only a few months. Bachmann provides numerous details (pp. 109-10); few will accuse her of anything except overzealousness in Christian duty after this book.

Bachmann describes in detail how she got started in politics (pp. 5-9). Bachmann fans might be surprised to learn that her first successful run for office was in 2000, for Minnesota State Senate (she ran unsuccessfully for School Board in 1999). She won her U.S. Congress seat in 2006, and hence is a relative newcomer only in her third term.

In other words, her political future looks long and bright: she is only 55 (which translates to at least three more possible presidential cycles); and she is one of the founders of the Tea Party movement. Her presidential run establishes Bachmann as one of the permanent leaders of the Tea Party; if they continue to do well, we can expect the same for Bachmann.

Book review written Dec. 2011;
full excerpts available online at:
www.ontheissues.org/Core_Conviction.htm

Book Review:
Michele Bachmann:
Why She Will Win
the Presidency in 2012
by Ron Paul Jones (June 8, 2011)

This is not really a "book" in the traditional sense: it's one of those new-fangled Internet books which are printed the day you buy it. That means it's very thin and very up-to-date. It feels more like a long magazine article with live updates.

This book was printed on June 8, the day I ordered it, and it already had updates on Libya (which occurred just a month or two before, a much shorter timeframe than is possible in traditionally-printed books). It also includes an up-to-the-minute list of opposing GOP candidates (which changes every week now).

The content of the book itself is a long editorial from a Bachmann fan. It addresses her strengths in the Republican primary and then in the general election against Pres. Obama. It has no criticism of Bachmann, and while it addresses her strong points, it ignores her weak points and hence is not the most meaningful analysis. But it's the only book on Bachmann currently available, and its new-media format makes it intriguing.

Book review written June 2011;
full excerpts available online at:
www.ontheissues.org/Why_She_Will_Win.htm

Book Review: America by Heart:
Reflections on Family, Faith, and Flag
by Gov. Sarah Palin (Nov. 23, 2010)

This book presents Sarah Palin's preparation for the 2012 presidential election. It summarizes her Talking Points on the issues, in the manner in which she will state them when running for president. Pundits accept that Going Rogue served as Palin's memoir of the 2008 race; this book instead is forward-looking. The book includes some biographical material—but mostly about topics which will be issues in the 2012 campaign. Those include:

- *Her daughter Bristol's teen pregnancy:* Palin deflects accusations of hypocrisy (i.e., she didn't sufficiently teach abstinence to her own daughter) by noting that those accusing her are admitting that she has principles, since hypocrisy implies non-adherence to principles. Discussing Bristol provides plenty of opportunity for discussing family values in general (besides appearing on "Dancing with the Stars," Bristol tours high schools telling other teens that abstinence would have served her better).

- *Her son Track's service in Iraq:* Palin finds numerous opportunities to glorify the American military; to glorify her son's selfless service to America; and to glorify the Stryker Brigade in which he serves. If you're into glorification of the military, you can expect a lot of it from Palin in 2012 based on this book.

- *Her infant son's Down Syndrome:* Palin discovered her son's affliction during pregnancy, and considers it a message from God that she and her husband Todd handle the difficulties which will follow. Politically, Palin gets the opportunity to apply her pro-life ethics and to describe those ethics in numerous related contexts.

However, the details of policy pale in importance compared to the style of the book: Palin positions herself as the female Ronald Reagan by imitating his folksy anecdotal style. Reagan famously kept a file of old clippings from popular magazines, which he quoted whenever asked for sources of his policy ideas (as lampooned in "Doonesbury," Reagan cited popular magazines like "The Reader's Digest" from the 1950s as sources of political wisdom).

Reagan also invented the ingenious method of introducing every major policy with an affected person (instead of just saying "We need policy X," Reagan would have an appropriate person in the audience and say, "Jane Doe suffers from Y and Z and demonstrates why we need policy X," while all the cameras would focus on a smiling Jane Doe).

Palin modernizes the down-home anecdote, or as she calls them in the introduction, "bits and pieces of Americana." She cites everything from the cartoon "The Incredibles" (p. 69) to the fictional character Jefferson Smith (the protagonist of "Mr. Smith Goes to Washington," p. 3), from the Reader's Digest (p. 45) to The Onion (a spoof newspaper, p. 99), to the Cowboy's Prayer (written by the first Poet Laureate of South Dakota, p. 231).

Flip through the book's pages and you'll find dozens of lengthy indented excerpts from sources such as John F. Kennedy (p. 70), Alexis de Tocqueville (p. 65), Margaret Thatcher (p. 133), and of course Ronald Reagan (p. 67 and more in our excerpts). And plenty of lesser luminaries and regular citizens as well, since Palin is no elitist who only cites Alexis de Tocqueville (and certainly this elitist reviewer was impressed that she could!).

These anecdotes, carefully documented and recorded in this book, will be called "inspirational" by her supporters and "sappy sentimentalism" by her detractors—and they will serve as Palin's standard stump responses to tough questions in the 2012 race.

In summary, this book is not so much a policy preview of 2012 as it is a stylistic preview. Palin is running, and running well. Her hit TV show "Sarah Palin's Alaska," is every political adviser's dream: free positive publicity over many months. And her 2010 endorsements (detailed in the chapter in this book on "Mama Grizzlies") mean she has plenty of political chits to cash in during the upcoming race, including several new members of the House and Senate. This book demonstrates that Palin's preparations for 2012 are well-considered and well under way.

Book review written Dec. 2010;
full excerpts available online at:
www.ontheissues.org/America_by_Heart.htm

Book Review: The Rogue:
Searching for the Real Sarah Palin, by Joe McGinnis (Sept. 20, 2010)

This is the book written by the guy who moved in next door to Sarah Palin. The author didn't originally intend the focus of the book to be his residence, but having moved in right next door in the summer of 2010, that became the focus of the book, and the focus of the controversy surrounding the book. Joe McGinnis, a supposedly legitimate political reporter who has published about Palin and about Alaska previously, originally intended the book as an investigation of Sarah's background and the people who knew her before the vice-presidential race.

But he stumbled upon the opportunity to move in next door to the Palins (by accident, he says on pp. 3-4). Hence several chapters are devoted to the Palin's reaction to discovering a hostile next-door neighbor, and to the national blowback (including hate-mails and death-threats) that resulted.

Ok, so getting past the silly next-door-neighbor issue, McGinnis' purpose is to elucidate Sarah Palin's true character by interviewing people who knew her well. But he only interviews people who didn't like Palin (admittedly, because those who DID like her wouldn't talk to the "stalker next door," as he points out on p. 207). Additional controversy about the book results from the even sillier issues that McGinnis raises as if they are legitimate political analysis:

- Sarah dated a black basketball player in college (how is this politically relevant? Glen Rice still speaks fondly of her; Sarah was not married at the time.) This gets a half a chapter and a photo on p. 25, where the author hints that Sarah is racist.

- Sarah is accused explicitly of being racist—not because she regretted dating Glen Rice, but because she didn't hire many minorities (p. 219). The author does mention—but does not diminish his accusations that Sarah is racist—that Sarah married a minority (Todd is part Native American).

- Sarah's daughter Bristol is suspected of being the actual mother of Sarah's Down syndrome baby—this warrants an entire chapter (e.g., p. 282) which evidently McGinnis hopes will blossom into a conspiracy theory based on the fact that Sarah looked trim even in her 7th month of pregnancy and other even less substantiated "facts."

- Todd has a dysfunctional family; Todd had extramarital affairs (p. 64) as did Sarah; Todd and Sarah have loud fights where they threaten divorce—while these topics would be fascinating cover stories for People magazine, they are not political reporting!

McGinnis loses all legitimacy as a political reporter, in our view, by bashing the mainstream media: "As America prepares for the 2012 presidential campaign, our mainstream media [is] reduced to a level of helpless codependency, in which its willing suspension of disbelief in regard to Sarah requires that it not look at or listen to her too closely, for fear that it might discover something it can't ignore." (p. 318). McGinnis doesn't get it—he IS the mainstream media! And he IS the problem—reporting on candidate's personal life as if it's news; "suspending disbelief" when any political enemy hints at some rumor or another; defining "something it can't ignore" as whether Sarah was a bully in grade school (p. 84). McGinnis fails in his duty as a reporter—this book is tabloid crap; fun to read for a little while, but not real political reporting.

We at OnTheIssues.org desired to explore Sarah Palin's background in the same manner that McGinnis claimed—by interviewing Wasilla residents who knew her in her mayoral days. We did so in a respectful manner in our 2008 interview of a Wasilla resident. If you want some meaningful background, read our interview—and throw McGinnis' book in the trash, where it belongs.

Book review written Oct. 2011;
full excerpts available online at:
www.ontheissues.org/The_Rogue.htm

Book Review: Going Rogue:
An American Life
by Gov. Sarah Palin (Nov. 17. 2009)

This book sent Palin on a nationwide book tour, including numerous media appearances which greatly raised her profile. The result of the book tour has established Palin as the frontrunner for the 2012 Republican presidential nomination. There's a long time until the election, but for now, Palin is more popular than Huckabee, Romney, Gingrich, and all the other likely prospects.

Since the 2008 campaign, Palin has been a polarizing figure, but some of that came from her assigned tasks in the McCain campaign. For example, she was assigned the task of delivering the campaign opinion on Bill Ayres, which was that Obama was "palling around with terrorists" (pp. 306-7), although Palin suggested then and now that McCain should have made more of the Ayers association. She also was the primary campaign spokesperson regarding "Joe the Plumber" (pp. 304-5), although she was certainly a willing and enthusiastic spokesperson, on that topic and on all polarizing issues. In other words,

Palin's polarization is well-deserved, and she seems to welcome the label. Palin does not, however, welcome media attacks on her, of which there are very many. This book gives Palin a chance to respond to the media attacks.

The title of the book comes from a McCain staffer who accused Palin of "going rogue," by giving her own opinion on issues on which the McCain campaign had not authorized her opinion. Palin is not one to withhold her opinions on anything, McCain's desires notwithstanding. Palin's book focuses on three of her most strongly-held opinions:

- *Energy:* Palin claims that Alaska can supply most of America's energy needs, if only we would "drill, baby, drill" (that's the title of Chapter Three). Prior to being governor, Palin was appointed as Alaska's Energy Czar; as governor, her proudest accomplishment was completing the AGIA project (a 1,700-mile gas pipeline, pp. 127-8 and 156-7). Energy is Palin's greatest passion; but she'll surprise environmentalists by having pushed a goal of 50% renewable electricity, a higher goal than Obama's 20% renewable target.

- **Guns:** Palin is equally impassioned about guns. We don't use the usual phrase "gun rights," because that's not her passion—it's guns themselves, or more specifically hunting and fishing. She refers to those activities repeatedly as obtaining "local organic protein sources," although one doubts that will seduce many vegetarians into voting for her. And she alienates vegetarians with phrases like "I love meat" (pp. 18-9, by which she means *hunting* for meat). Palin includes lots of pictures of her bagging moose; skinning fish; and enough to indicate it's not just for photo ops.

- **Ethics:** Government ethics is Palin's professional passion—it's how she got elected, having ousted the incumbent Republican governor on grounds of questionable ethics (pp. 112-3) after having resigned as Energy Czar on grounds of the energy agency's bad ethics (pp. 96-9). Palin's focus on ethics, and campaign reform, and government transparency, and so on, is the reason McCain chose her for V.P., since McCain has the same focus.

- **Religion:** This is *not* Palin's passion—although the media portrays Palin as if she were a Jesus-freak. She's certainly proudly a Christian, and pro-life and anti-evolution and all the other stances that implies, but she focuses her attention and her basis for policy decisions elsewhere. Typical of her attitude is how she met her husband Todd: she describes him as a cussin' non-church-goer, but acceptable because he had been baptized (pp. 33-7). McCain's other reason for choosing Palin as V.P. was that she brought with her an army of a million Christian conservative volunteers. The Christian conservative movement adores Palin, but for those who want a preacher, Mike Huckabee is their candidate, not Palin.

Democrats may reconsider their low opinion of Palin after reading this book—if not on policy grounds, then on grounds of her book tour popularity. OnTheIssues.org recognizes Palin's popularity because the day she was nominated, we received 835,000 viewers, the most of any day in our history. We also recognize Palin's political accomplishments—she took on the Republican establishment head-on and beat them, in the one-party state of Republican Alaska. I'm a progressive in Massachusetts, another one-party state in which the establishment party deplores us as outsiders, and Palin accomplished what it has taken a movement in Massachusetts a decade to do. She has earned her place as a political leader; read this book to get her side of the story!

Book review written Nov. 2009;
full excerpts available online at:
www.ontheissues.org/Going_Rogue.htm

Bachmann vs. Palin
on VoteMatch

VoteMatch is our 20-question quiz which summarizes the candidate's views on the controversial issues of the day.

VoteMatch Social Issues

	Bachmann	Palin
Abortion is a woman's right	strongly opposes	opposes
Require companies to hire more women & minorities	opposes	favors
Same-sex domestic partnership benefits	strongly opposes	opposes
Teacher-led prayer in public schools	strongly favors	strongly favors
Parents choose schools via vouchers	strongly favors	strongly favors

VoteMatch Domestic Issues

	Bachmann	Palin
More federal funding for health coverage	strongly opposes	opposes
Death Penalty	neutral	strongly favors
Mandatory Three Strikes sentencing laws	opposes	strongly favors
Absolute right to gun ownership	strongly favors	strongly favors
Drug use is immoral: enforce laws against it	opposes	favors

VoteMatch Economic Issues

	Bachmann	Palin
Privatize Social Security	strongly favors	opposes
Make taxes more progressive	strongly opposes	opposes
Stricter limits on political campaign funds	strongly favors	strongly favors
Allow churches to provide welfare services	favors	favors
Replace coal & oil with alternatives	strongly opposes	opposes

VoteMatch International Issues

	Bachmann	Palin
Illegal immigrants earn citizenship	strongly opposes	favors
Support & expand free trade	favors	favors
The Patriot Act harms civil liberties	strongly opposes	opposes
Expand the armed forces	favors	strongly favors
US out of Iraq & Afghanistan	strongly opposes	opposes

In our online quiz, you fill in your answers for these 20 questions, and we match you against all the candidates. Please see:

http://quiz.ontheissues.org/

Afterword

We hope that this book encourages you, as voters, to make your decisions based on the issues. We recognize the reality of American politics: voters make their decisions based primarily on whether they like the candidates. Accordingly, our goal is to get voters to compare their issue preferences in comparison to candidate issue stances when considering which candidates to like.

We intentionally omitted from this book any biographical background on Rep. Bachmann and Speaker Palin. Details of their birthplaces and religious affiliations—and minutiae of every other personal detail—are readily available in the mainstream media. Their issue stances are more challenging for voters to find.

Why does the mainstream media fail at this important function? Because they are "news" organizations which are poorly suited to covering political campaigns. "News" implies reporting on what is "new": Palin's stance on the War on Drugs has not changed since 1998, and Bachmann's stance on the Gold standard has not changed since 1981, so there's nothing in the news about those issues. But if you are impassioned about the Drug War, or if you vote based on Fed policy, then you cannot rely on the news media for those non-newsworthy issues. And that's where we come in.

This book represents an archive of where these two candidates stand on the key issues of our time. We don't consider whether candidates' issue stances are new—just what they say on each issue. That often requires a lot of digging on our part—we have a team of researchers to do that, but we invite you to volunteer any issue stances that we don't cover.

Our online website www.ontheissues.org covers many more issues than can fit in any book: many more stances from Romney and Perry, as well as all of the other 2012 candidates, Governors, Senators, and House members. We score each candidate on a 20-question quiz called "VoteMatch." A representation of the VoteMatch quiz results for the presidential contenders appears on the back cover of this book. The mainstream media interpret candidates using a one-dimensional "right-left" analysis. That simplistic analysis comes to nonsensical conclusions like calling Michele Bachmann "extreme right-wing" even though he opposes the Iraq War; opposes the PATRIOT Act; supports drug legalization; and supports same-sex domestic partnership benefits.

We find our two-dimensional analysis to be more accurate in differentiating candidates than that traditional one-dimensional analysis. We don't claim that our method is perfect—just superior to the simplistic mainstream media. VoteMatch uses a Social Issues dimension plus an Economic Issues dimension; we interpret candidates based on whether they believe in government involvement in either or both of those dimensions. Using the two-dimensional analysis differentiates five classes of political beliefs:

1. *Libertarian:*
   No government involvement in social issues
   No government involvement in economic issues

2. *Conservative:*
   Government involvement in social issues
   No government involvement in economic issues

3. *Liberal:*
   No government involvement in social issues
   Government involvement in economic issues

4. *Populist:*
   Government involvement in social issues
   Government involvement in economic issues

5. *Centrist:*
   Some government involvement in social issues
   Some government involvement in economic issues

Most importantly, you can answer the same 20 questions and see *your* political label and how the candidates match up with *you*. We invite you to try the VoteMatch quiz at:

http://quiz.ontheissues.org

Other Books in This Series

- Rick Perry vs. Mitt Romney On The Issues

- Barack Obama vs. Hillary Clinton On The Issues

- Newt Gingrich vs. Ron Paul On The Issues

About the Author

Jesse Gordon has been the editor-in-chief of OnTheIssues.org since its formation in 1999. His passion revolves around providing issue-based coverage on political races, to combat the mainstream media's growing lack of such coverage.

Mr. Gordon holds a Master's degree in Public Policy from Harvard University's Kennedy School of Government. He and the website OnTheIssues.org are based in Cambridge, Massachusetts. He resides with his fiancée, Kathleen; his son Julien; Kathleen's son Derek; their cat Chanel; and six fish with whom Chanel is obsessed.

Mr. Gordon replies to email personally, at jesse@ontheissues. org—whether to suggest improvements to the website or to order one of the other books above.

CPSIA information can be obtained at www.ICGtesting.com
Printed in the USA
BVOW02s1844151015

422719BV00001B/15/P

9 781468 127195